S0-BSJ-280

SIX GREAT PLAYWRIGHTS

In the same Series

SIX GREAT ACTORS	Richard Findlater
SIX GREAT AMERICANS	Kenneth M. King
SIX GREAT ARCHITECTS	Robert Lutyens
SIX GREAT AVIATORS	John Pudney
SIX GREAT CHRISTIANS	Peggy Chambers
SIX GREAT COMPOSERS	John Warrack
SIX GREAT DANCERS	Mary Clarke
SIX GREAT DOCTORS	J. G. Crowther
SIX GREAT ENGINEERS	J. G. Crowther
SIX GREAT ENGLISHMEN	Aubrey de Sélincourt
SIX GREAT ENGLISHWOMEN	Yvonne ffrench
SIX GREAT EXPLORERS	David Divine
SIX GREAT INVENTORS	J. G. Crowther
SIX GREAT MISSIONARIES	Phyllis Garlick
SIX GREAT MOUNTAINEERS	Ronald W. Clark
SIX GREAT NATURALISTS	R. S. R. Fitter
SIX GREAT NOVELISTS	Walter Allen
SIX GREAT PAINTERS	Michael Levey
SIX GREAT POETS	Aubrey de Sélincourt
SIX GREAT RAILWAYMEN	Richard Hough
SIX GREAT SAILORS	David Divine
SIX GREAT SCIENTISTS	J. G. Crowther
SIX GREAT THINKERS	Aubrey de Sélincourt

SIX GREAT PLAYWRIGHTS

SOPHOCLES . SHAKESPEARE . MOLIÈRE
SHERIDAN . IBSEN . SHAW

BY
AUBREY DE SELINCOURT

HAMISH HAMILTON
LONDON

First published in Great Britain 1960
by Hamish Hamilton Ltd
90 *Great Russell Street London W.C.*1

PRINTED IN GREAT BRITAIN
BY WESTERN PRINTING SERVICES LTD. BRISTOL

To Belos

who read this book in manuscript
and helped me with her criticism and advice,
with my love

A. de S.

CONTENTS

ILLUSTRATIONS

FOREWORD

THERE is a certain presumptuousness in attempting to write of the work of such men as Shakespeare, Sophocles and Molière, and even of such as my other three, within the narrow compass which a book like this allows. To most of them libraries of print have been devoted, and one might well suppose that everything worth saying, amongst much which was not, has already been said, save for specialist studies on one or another neglected aspect of them. I need hardly say that these sketches of mine are in no way specialist studies; nor do they make any claim to shed what is called 'new light' upon their subjects. If the pictures I have given are in fact new in any way at all, either in colour or emphasis or design, that is simply because they have been drawn by me, and not by anyone else; for I have tried to approach each of my playwrights freshly, as if for the first time, and to record, in the capacity not of a scholar but of a common reader, as indeed I am, what has struck me as most vital and important in their work.

The choice of six out of all the playwrights of the world was not an easy one. Shakespeare, no doubt, had to be one of them, though in choosing even him I found myself in some embarrassment, as in my earlier book *Six Great Poets* I had refused to include him on the ground that anyone who fancied he could be interesting about Shakespeare at this late date in the space at my disposal was either arrogant or stupid. But I could not refuse twice; so he has gone in, and I have done the best I can.

As to the others, I wanted to spread the net as wide as possible and not to confine myself to writers in English; and I wanted, at the same time—and this, I think, is important—to write only of men whose language I have some knowledge of. Being myself a translator, I mistrust translations. One Greek I had to have, and the fairly obvious choice was Sophocles, as Aeschylus is too craggy and difficult for the lay reader, Aristophanes too full of esoteric jokes, while Euripides is not really representative of his age or civilization, being a brilliant experimenter and iconoclast, feeling his way towards a new kind of drama. The French choice was easy, Molière's plays being incomparably the richest in humanity of any that France has produced, besides being more readily enjoyed than any others by the British peoples.

By including Ibsen I deserted one of my principles, for I know nothing of the Norse language. This is a serious disqualification for writing about him, as I am well aware; nevertheless I could not leave him out, his influence upon European drama having been so great, even apart from the intrinsic quality of his work. Moreover Ibsen has for so long been familiar to British playgoers that we almost forget that the words we hear from the stage were not his own.

Sheridan and Shaw may need some justification. For Sheridan I have given it to the best of my ability in the course of my essay; as for Shaw, I wanted a modern—or a near-modern—and Shaw seemed the most suitable choice. Most of our actual contemporaries either bewilder or repel me, and I could not write of them; besides, it takes time even for the finest writer to become 'great': opinion has to settle, and he has to be seen from a little distance, in the context of his age. I do not know if future ages will admit that Shaw is great; probably not; but at any rate he was great *fun*, and a brilliantly intelligent playwright who, like Ibsen whom he so much admired, had an important and, on the whole, a beneficent, influence on English drama.

The series in which this book appears was designed to interest young, or youngish, readers. This is a fairly vague category; so, as my subject is not an elementary one, and Sophocles and Ibsen can hardly be considered food for babes, I have tried to write what I know from long experience would have been interesting and useful to my own pupils in the upper forms of various schools. I have made no attempt to temper the wind, having further learned that to do so alienates *all* readers, whatever their age or experience.

Great plays, like great poems or novels, are readings of life; and I have tried wherever it was possible to suggest the implicit philosophical content of the plays I have discussed, as well as their more obvious dramatic power. I hope this may help my less experienced readers to form for themselves certain standards of judgement, which they will be able to apply to their reading generally—and which I think are more than ever necessary in the welter of contemporary literature.

I

SOPHOCLES
496–405 B.C.

OUGHT a reasonably intelligent person to be able, when confronted with an acknowledged masterpiece of art, to understand and appreciate it without previous knowledge of the circumstances in which it was produced? In other words, is beauty—or whatever else one takes to be the informing spirit of a work of art—'autonomous'—does it, that is, exist as something in its own right, independently, so that to see it is to recognize it, or is it, on the contrary, a somewhat mysterious end-product of a thousand other things subtly combined and each modifying all the rest?

I would suggest that the latter is more nearly the truth, and to back my view I would point to the obvious fact that all art is, and must be, built upon certain conventions. It is a way of communicating, and nobody can communicate with another person without some common ground. A visitor from Mars might well be puzzled by the ninth symphony of Beethoven, or by *King Lear* or by *Paradise Lost*—and it would be unjust to call him stupid. We tend in the matter of the arts, as in most other matters, to like what we are used to and to be irked by the unfamiliar. Writers and artists draw into a focus, like a lens, the diffused light of thought and feeling characteristic of their time, making their contemporaries know clearly what they half-knew already, or dimly guessed, or caught fugitive glimpses of. They see what others see, but they see it better. Often they are a jump ahead, and in times of change catch and draw into their focus ideas which are only faintly beginning to stir on the outermost edge of the general consciousness, so that what they say seems difficult and strange, till the gap has been narrowed; but the ideas are there, however nebulous.

For these reasons it is not possible, I think, to understand the literature of the past unless one has some knowledge of the conventions—of the accepted ways, that is, of thinking and feeling—out of which it sprang. It is no good, for instance, to shy away from the poetry of Pope because it contains no awareness of our modern solicitude for the humble and obscure—or of Wordsworth's solicitude for the Betty Foys of the world, or children who take their little porringers and eat their supper in the churchyard. Even *with* knowledge of the conventions, it is difficult to understand completely the literature of another age than our own, because to know how people felt about things is not the same by any means as feeling that way ourselves. It seems, therefore, that there must always be a veil, sometimes thin, sometimes less thin, between us and the literature of other ages; and this would be discouraging, were it not for another fact of the first importance—namely that great writers always transcend the conventions within which they write; their doing so is precisely the thing in which their greatness consists, and in them those very conventions come to appear simply as a means to an end beyond themselves. To Milton, for instance, the theology of *Paradise Lost* was vital, and I do not think we can understand the poem without understanding the theology; but we love the poem for a different reason: we love it—some of us—because Milton, being a great poet, transcended his argument and was able through the power and magnificence of his tremendous story, to tell us things about the laws of life in this world which are true for all men in all ages, regardless of creed: that freedom, for instance, is necessarily involved in obedience to law, a truth which the pagan Sophocles would have been as ready to accept—and did, in fact, constantly express—as any Christian, Moslem or Jew.

It is necessary, I think, to begin with a general caution of this sort, because an English reader today, coming direct to an ancient Greek drama with no knowledge of the conventions from which it sprang or of the quality of thought and feeling to which it was originally addressed, is not likely to make much of it; and this would be a loss, as ancient Greek literature is the finest in the world after our own, and of that literature the tragic drama is the crown.

In approaching Greek plays most of the ideas which we associate with 'the theatre' are irrelevant. Athenian drama had its origin in religion, and the production of plays was a part of the ritual worship of Dionysus, god of vegetation, fertility and wine. Plays were exhibited only at the annual festivals of Dionysus, of which the most important was the City Dionysia, in early spring, when Athens was full of visitors from other states, bent on business or pleasure. The festival was a public holiday; shops were closed, the courts were emptied, no business of any kind was transacted—even prisoners were released from gaol—and for four days—possibly for five—the whole population of Athens crowded to the great open-air theatre (it held from 17,000 to 20,000 people) at the foot of the Acropolis and sat there from dawn to dusk to watch a succession of plays, tragedy and comedy, and to listen to the choral singing of hymns in honour of Dionysus. The first day was devoted to a grand Procession; an ancient statue of the God was taken from its shrine and carried along the road to Eleutherae, a town on the Boeotian border from which it was supposed to have been originally brought; and then, in the evening, it was brought back by torchlight and set up, not in its shrine, but in the theatre, to preside over the spectacles to come. All the City, men, women and children, turned out in holiday dress for the procession—solemn in import, but a gay and brilliant spectacle with the companies of young citizen soldiers escorting, in full armour, the sacred image, the long lines of garlanded animals, victims for the sacrifice, following behind, the girls carrying on their heads the baskets containing the sacrificial implements, and the City magistrates robed in purple or crowned with gold. The theatre itself was a sacred building, and misbehaviour of any sort within it was looked upon as sacrilege: merely to turn a man out of a seat which did not belong to him was an offence punishable with death.

It sounds a solemn business—and so it was, in so far as the whole Festival was an act of worship; but at the same time it was an occasion for pleasure beyond any other that the course of the year provided. The Greeks lived closer to death than we do—and for that reason, perhaps, swallowed life with a sharper appetite. They had not explained Nature away, as we, in our smugger moments, fancy we have done; for them Nature was still ultimately inscrutable—and hostile. She would get you if she could—or the gods would get you, for the gods were projections of various forces and tendencies in nature, many of them malignant, and also of certain deep and powerful urges within the human spirit: of love, for instance (always in Greek thought the Destroyer), of Revenge, of Remorse, of irrational Terror (panic, from Pan) in lonely places. And there was a queer something called Fate, or Necessity, another irrational, and awful, power superior even to Zeus, the king of the gods. It was necessary for a Greek to get the gods *on his side*: to propitiate them; to ignore them, or to act as if one were independent of them, was not wicked so much as foolish; for such conduct led inevitably to ruin. Thus Greek religion, not only the darker side of it which I have just suggested, but also the innumerable local sanctities and the 'happy pieties' connected with every commonest action of life from day to day and hour to hour, was woven into the very stuff of consciousness. The Greeks had no Sunday; and they made no connection in their minds between religion and goodness. All Greeks were religious, but by no means all Greeks were good. Their commonest term for 'goodness' in its most general moral sense was *sophron* a word which was applied to people who 'knew their place' and did not get above themselves either in human relationships or in their attitude towards those mysterious powers which demand humility from man.

Since, then, there was in Greek feeling no hard dividing line between the secular and the 'sacred', it is not difficult to see how the great religious festival of the Dionysia could be, at the same time, a tremendous jamboree. Except at such festivals the Greeks were starved of anything that could be called public entertainment; an exceedingly quick-witted people, with few books, no newspapers or concerts, no theatres as we know them, an unspoiled taste and the keenest of appetites for any sort of spectacle, they looked forward to their annual shows with passionate expectancy, and—the ignorant and the educated alike—packed tight on their comfortless wooden benches (the stone theatre in Athens was built after Sophocles' time) sat happily through the long daylight hours watching plays which have never been surpassed for subtlety of thought and language, grandeur of feeling and lyrical magnificence. A Greek play is supposed to be meat for the highbrows nowadays—but how a Greek would have laughed at that ridiculous word! If the Greeks wanted plays, they wanted *good* plays—and that was all there was to it; they had not made the lamentable distinction between entertainment for the masses and entertainment for the elect. They had, moreover, at all their dramatic festivals, the further interest and excitement of competition: the plays were staged competitively, judged by a carefully selected board of judges, and the winning author was awarded a prize. The prize, not of much intrinsic value, was nevertheless one of the highest civic honours, the poet (as he was called, not the 'playwright') being looked upon not only as the provider of entertainment but as the teacher of wisdom.

Greek drama was the development of a primitive religious ritual in which a group of worshippers sang, with appropriate movements and gestures, a choral hymn in honour of the god. The dance and the hymn were performed on a circular enclosure called an 'orchestra', or 'dancing-place'. Later the simple rite was elaborated by the introduction of a single actor—the Greeks called him an 'answerer'—whose function was to punctuate, or comment upon, or 'answer' the phases of the choral hymn. In this the germ of dramatic representation can already be seen. How ancient this ritual was, nobody knows, but early in the fifth century before Christ the poet Aeschylus first introduced a second actor and thus made dialogue possible. It was the decisive step forward to the creation of drama. At the same time the ritual nature of the performance remained; the choral hymns were still the centre of it. Even in Aeschylus' three most elaborate and magnificent plays—the trilogy or connected series, which tell the story of the curse on the house of Atreus—though in the wild prophesyings of Cassandra and the maniac and devoted rage of Clytemnestra the murderess there is indeed drama as we understand the word, the essence of the whole is still in the choral hymns, those dark, intense, brooding poems on the mystery of evil and the helplessness of man before a power, malignant and inexorable, which he can guess at but never understand.

It is the chorus, I think, which to a modern reader gives the greatest sense of strangeness in a Greek play and is most likely to spoil his understanding of it; but the difficulty can be overcome if one realizes why the chorus was originally there, and holds fast to the fact that Greek drama, in origin a religious ritual, kept the ritual form throughout its history. The work of Sophocles was to modify that form and so to bring the drama one step—a long one—nearer to what we understand by it today. This he did by two apparently simple devices: he reduced the importance of the chorus, and he introduced a third actor, thus making possible, by the interplay of dialogue, dramatic situations more numerous and varied, and a subtler presentation of character and motive.

Sophocles was born at the village of Colonus, a mile or so outside Athens, in 496 B.C. Thus he was a child of six when the news was brought to Athens of the defeat of Darius' army at Marathon. He died at the age of ninety, when the bitter, thirty years' war between Athens and Sparta was nearing its end. It was a fortunate period to live in—the one great century of the flowering of Athenian civilization. Very few facts are known of Sophocles' personal life: his father, a well-to-do metal-worker, or perhaps owner of a factory in which weapons were made, gave him the best education of the time and an entry into good society; at the age of fifteen he was chosen to lead the boys' chorus which sang the Paean in thanksgiving for the defeat of the Persian navy at Salamis; he won his first victory at the Dionysia with a play written when he was twenty-eight; on one occasion at least he commanded the citizen army, but was said neither to know nor care much about public business 'except as befitted a decent Athenian'. He was a friend of Herodotus and of Pericles, and certainly knew Socrates, though one can guess that he did not always see eye to eye with him. He continued to write until the very end of his long life, and—if we are right in believing *Oedipus at Colonus* to be his last play—with increasing power. Two lines of verse in the Greek *Anthology* inform us that he died 'eating a bunch of Bacchus' grapes'—a statement which some people, including myself, interpret as meaning not that he choked himself with a pip, but was engaged at the time of his death on another play. Even Greek poetry can be fanciful at times and does not always call a spade a spade.

Sophocles wrote in all over a hundred plays, of which seven survive. There is a pleasant story, told by various ancient writers, of the poet in extreme old age: the version of the essayist Lucian is as follows. 'Towards the end of his life, having been brought into the courts by his son Iophon on a charge of mental incompetence due to senility, he read to the jury some passages from the *Oedipus at Colonus*; this proved the continued vigour of his intellect to such effect that the jury were filled with admiration of him, and condemned Iophon, instead, as a lunatic.'

Apart from the ritual form of which I have already spoken, Greek tragic drama differed from modern in another important particular: the subjects of the plays were always (there is only one extant exception, *The Persians* of Aeschlyus) taken from ancient heroic legend or myth. These old stories were pretty certainly accepted by most Greeks as historical fact, whether they were stories about gods or about 'heroes'—those shadowy primeval figures, larger than life, whose exploits were celebrated in the poems of Homer and elsewhere in the great mass of saga and song which was as familiar to an Athenian of the fifth century as the Bible is to us. But the point is that these stories were *known*; and a Greek audience at a play would not, therefore, have had the pleasure and excitement of wondering *what was going to happen*, for that was decided already; their pleasure and excitement came from another cause—from the particular handling, namely, of the familiar theme and from the playwright's ability to bring it home to them as an image (which all good stories are) of human struggle and human destiny. This Sophocles achieved partly by the delineation of character, but chiefly by the sheer power and magic of poetry.

Now the fact that it is the poetry which makes a play of Sophocles, or of any other Greek tragic writer, what it is presents two difficulties to anyone who would attempt to introduce such plays to a modern reader unacquainted with Greek: first, poetry cannot be translated. The bones of it can be translated; but poetry does not consist only of bones. The spirit of it, and even the flesh, vanishes in translation. Secondly, the present day is, I think, in the main antipathetic to poetic drama, which requires broad themes and a certain boldness of treatment rather than the burrowing, minute psychological analysis of the novel, which is the characteristic literary form of the modern world. We enjoy burrowing nowadays and are apt to applaud the novelist who with indefatigable industry traces the failure of Mr. X to live on comfortable terms with his wife to the fact that somebody said Boo to him when he was a baby. But poetic drama takes the great commonplaces of human experience, and transfigures them. Shakespeare's tragic themes were ambition, pride, infatuation, jealousy, and it was his poetry which subtilized and illuminated them; Othello without his poetry would be nothing less trite than a jealous husband; but the poetry reveals his glory as well as his shame. Sophocles' tragic themes were the Great Man Fallen, the conflict between private affection and public duty, inescapable destiny, submission to God's laws, the darkness which lies in wait for the passion and splendour of man's brief life—and again it is his poetry which brings them home to us. Without the poetry they would be nothing—or little more than dramatized homilies.

The order in which Sophocles' seven surviving plays were written cannot be exactly determined; but probably *Ajax* was the earliest. Ajax was the great Fighter, second only amongst the Greeks who fought at Troy to Achilles. According to the legend, when Achilles died and the question arose to whom his armour should be given, the Greek captains, led by Agamemnon and Menelaus, awarded it not to Ajax but to Odysseus. Ajax in the rage of wounded pride swore to murder them all, but the goddess Athene, always Odysseus' friend, turned the wits of Ajax so that in the darkness of hallucination he killed the army's cattle, supposing them to be his enemies. The deed done, he came to his senses again, and in shame killed himself. What a story! Looked at with detachment, the cattle-killing comes very near to the ludicrous, and for English readers at any rate the inability of a brave man to accept the hurt to his pride with any sort of dignity is not easy to tolerate. However, poets have a way with unpromising material; they bewitch us more surely even than Athene bewitched Ajax; they suspend our disbelief, make us see what isn't there (like Macbeth's air-drawn dagger) and involve us in their fantasies. The result is that, reading this play, we do *not* look at the improbable story with detachment but are drawn within it and forced to realize, against all the evidence of the facts, that the insufferable Ajax has a demonic power in him and a sort of awful greatness; and that realization casts, in its turn, a lurid light—or call it perhaps a 'darkness visible', like the flames in Milton's hell—upon certain places of the human heart. Man, we feel when the last page is turned, even though the gods drive him mad, is greater than we know.

Sophocles achieves his effect in this play chiefly by two great scenes: the first is where Ajax, having returned to his right mind, sees before him the one inevitable thing that he must do. He has made a fool of himself, and ridicule to a Greek was worse than any pain. Honour must be saved, and it can be saved only by death. To find that death, he must be alone, so he tells the seamen who have followed him to the war from his home in the island of Salamis and his slave-wife Tecmessa that he is going to the sea-shore to some lonely spot where he may wash himself clean of the stain of his offence:

I will go now to the seaward grasslands and the waters
To wash the stain and be free at last of Athene's anger;
I will find some place where no foot has trod
And there I will hide this sword of mine, this hated sword,
Burying it in the ground where no man may see it—
Deep down there night and Hell shall keep it for me,
For since I took it as a gift from Hector who hated me
Never have the Greeks honoured me as I deserved.
Ah! it is a true word that says an enemy's gift
Is no gift and brings with it only sorrow!
Therefore I will learn henceforward to be humble towards God,
And obedient to Atreus' sons. For they are
My captains, so how should I gainsay them?
Wild things, the mightiest things, yield to authority—
The snows and gales of winter give place to summer's fruits,
The dismal eye of night to the white horses of dawn bringing the daylight,
The tempest's terrible breath lulls at last the sighing sea,
And invincible sleep looses whom he has bound.
How then shall I too not learn to curb my pride?

For nothing remains in a fixed stay, and even friendship
Is a treacherous harbour for most of us . . .
Wife, go you within
And pray God that what my heart longs for may be done.
And you, friends, honour her even as you honour me
And bid my brother, if he comes, be kind to you, and
tend me
According to my need—for I go whither I must go.
Only obey me, and perhaps, though I suffer now,
You will soon find me safe enough.

His friends are unaware of the many ironies in these words: they do not guess *how* he will bury his sword, how he will curb his pride, what it is his heart longs for. With joy for their master's imagined recovery and repentance they let him go. A messenger enters with the news of a prophecy that Ajax is in deadly danger, but that if he is guarded today he will henceforward be safe. Tecmessa and the sailors scatter to search for him —but they are too late. The scene changes to the 'seaward grasslands', and Ajax is alone. He has buried the hilt of Hector's great sword in the ground, and the blade is upward.

There stands the Butcher, where most aptly he can cut
The victim's throat . . . fixed he is in the earth of Troy,
My enemy; the whetstone has ground his iron to a
bright new edge,
And I have stamped the earth hard, to make him kind
to me
With a swift death. It is well done.
And now, O Zeus, do not turn from me, but grant me
One boon, a little boon—that some messenger may bear
The ill word to my brother Teucer, to bring him quickly
That he may be the first to lift me and draw out the
bloody blade,

Before some enemy sees my body and throws it out
To be eaten by birds and dogs . . . And you, O
ghost-guide Hermes,
Put me to sleep without a struggle—with one swift leap
Upon the sword-point bursting my side. And I call the
Avengers,
The maiden ones, the hastening Furies, whose eye
no mortal pain escapes,
To witness that it is Atreus' sons who kill me now,
And to sweep them to as bitter a death as mine. . . .
Sun, who drive your chariot up the steep sky,
When you see my home, check your golden reins and tell
My father and her who nursed me to sorrow
Of my miserable end.
Death, Death, draw near and look at me—
Yet there, whither I go, we shall be close and I shall
talk with you.
Daylight and sun—O bright one, O charioteer—
Once more I call your names, for the last time—never
again.
Sky-brightness, and you, O holy earth of Salamis,
My home; famous Athens, and all springs and streams
Which here in Troy's plains have fed my life, hail and
farewell!
This is the last word that I speak to you—the rest
I shall tell
Only to the dead in the dark world below.

Teucer comes—and Ajax is indeed 'safe enough'; he has gone 'whither he had to go'. If a brave man must kill himself for shame, that, I suppose, is how he should do it; if he must humble himself before God, he could not do so with more fitting pride. Ajax dies as he has lived, proud, unyielding, still full of revengeful thoughts. Do we grieve for him? I think not; rather we are brought face to face with the tragic fact of human destiny, of the closeness of death and the impotence of human strength which make the 'sky-brightness and all springs and streams' the dearer for the brief time that they are ours. At the end of the play Teucer tells Ajax' son, the boy Eurysaces, to help him lift his father's body, 'for still,' he says, 'the hot veins are pouring the black strength up from his heart.' What an image of the invincible fighter, of the fierce physical life not yet wholly subdued! and reading the words one remembers Odysseus, in the first scene, when Athene has allowed him to see the madman in his tent:

> 'I weep for his distress
> Though he is my enemy; seeing his lot surely I see my own;
> For now I know that we men are indeed nothing
> But phantoms, or a shadow bodiless as air.'

I have spoken at some length about this play which, though not the best that Sophocles wrote, is yet a noble play, because being comparatively simple in theme and construction it offers, I think, a very clear example of the quality and kind of Sophocles' art—so different from that of any modern playwright. It is easy to recognize in it the sheer poetic and imaginative power which turns the old, dark legend into an image of the human condition—of Man who in the pride of his own blazing physical life forgets the eternal law and makes his very zest for living the means of his destruction. 'Seeing these things,' says the goddess Athene to Odysseus,

> Speak no proud word against God
> Or think yourself big because you are rich or strong;
> There is nothing a man has but a day can bring it down
> And lift it up again. Those who know their place and are humble
> Are the ones God loves.

In *Ajax* there is no character-drawing in our sense of the term. The figures are ideal figures. Up to a point this is true of all Sophocles' plays, though some people have tried to believe that it is not. No character in Sophocles speaks with an individual accent; there is no equivalent in him, to say, Falstaff or Hamlet or Hotspur or Rosalind or Iago, whose very *voices* we know. Indeed such character-drawing as that is foreign to the spirit of ancient drama, partly because of its ritual form and partly, no doubt, because of the physical conditions under which it was presented. The enormous size of the theatre, and the fact that the actors wore masks and increased their height by thick-soled shoes would preclude much of the subtle by-play of dialogue and expression by which a sense of individual character is built up. Greek playwrights worked in masses; their lines, one guesses, were declaimed rather than spoken, and under their sculptured forms beat the hearts not of men, but of Man. Nevertheless Sophocles in his later plays did take a step towards what one might call a more modern feeling for characterization—or at least opened a gate on to a new path which subsequent playwrights were to follow. Some people have put it much more strongly and have claimed Antigone, for instance (in the play of that name) as a piece of consummate characterization; but though in her devotion to the dictates of her heart she yet weeps for the loss of life and of love, to try to see her as something other than a symbolic figure of profound moral and emotional significance is to misread the intention of the play and of Sophocles' art as a whole.

I suppose *Antigone* is the best loved today of Sophocles' plays; the reason is obvious, for the theme it treats is easier than that of any of the other plays for a modern reader to understand. It is less craggy and remote and more obviously human, and therefore engages our sympathies with a slighter demand upon our imagination. Superficially, anyone could enjoy it, as—superficially—anyone could enjoy *Hamlet*; nevertheless it is only the theme which makes concessions; its total significance as a work of art, and the resonances of its poetry, call not for less but for more awareness than the simpler *Ajax*.

The two sons of Oedipus, Eteocles and Polynices, ruled together over the city of Thebes. Quarrels arose between them, and Eteocles banished his brother who, in revenge, gathered a foreign army and marched against his native city. The foreign champions were defeated, but, in the final combat between the brothers, each fell by the other's hand. Creon, the successor to the throne of Thebes, issued a proclamation that Eteocles should have an honourable burial as defender of the city, but that the body of Polynices, who had attempted its destruction, should be flung out to be eaten by scavenging beasts and birds, the penalty of death being denounced upon anyone who should perform the rites of burial for the traitor. At this point in the story the play of *Antigone* begins.

Antigone, who is the sister of Polynices and loved him, determines to flout Creon's proclamation and, with full knowledge of the consequences to herself, to sprinkle the ritual dust upon her brother's body and so save his ghost from what, to a Greek, was one of the worst of horrors. This she does, her more timid sister Ismene having refused to help her. The act is discovered—she has made no attempt to conceal it—and she is buried alive in a vault. Her lover Haemon, Creon's son, appeals for her in vain; Creon is adamant, until the blind seer Teiresias prophecies disaster as a result of his excessive severity—first to the brother, then to the sister. He weakens and hesitates, then decides to revoke his decisions. He buries Polynices, then goes to the vault to release Antigone, but arrives too late. Antigone has hanged herself with strips of her own clothing, and Haemon has already forced his way into the chamber and has his arms round his lover's body. Seeing Creon he makes for him with his sword; but Creon escapes and Haemon kills himself. To make up the tale of woe, Creon's wife Eurydice, hearing of Haemon's death, also dies by her own hand. Not, one would say, a plot without incident.

With such a splendid abundance of corpses I suppose it might have been possible even for a very stupid Greek to enjoy this play simply for the story, just as a very stupid Englishman can enjoy *Hamlet*, with its seven violent deaths, its fight in an open grave, its ghost and its escape from pirates, simply as a rousing melodrama. And it is true that Sophocles, like Shakespeare, manages his melodramatics with great skill. But—again like Shakespeare—Sophocles was a poet, and it is the office of poetry to start in us 'thoughts beyond the reaches of our souls'. Like the *Ajax*, though much subtler and ampler in treatment, the *Antigone* is a complex image of human destiny, conceived on a high religious—which to a Greek would not differ from a high poetic, or philosophical—plane. It is instinct with the dark fatalism characteristic of Sophocles, and perhaps of most Greeks of his time: a kind of unresentful pessimism which in no way takes the colour and glory from life—while it lasts—and is therefore so different from the pessimism widely current in the modern world, which seeks to turn life itself to ashes. For Sophocles Man is indeed born to sorrow: the inscrutable gods have ordained it, though, being what he is—passionate, ignorant, proud—he moves towards it of his own act and by his own will. Is there a contradiction here? Perhaps there is, though it did not appear so to Sophocles, who, in any case, was not a metaphysician but a poet. Much of the power and *weight* of the *Antigone* comes from the fact that the story is part of one of the many Greek legends which concern the curse on a particular family. The family of Oedipus was one such, and it is not hard to see the imaginative use which can be made of such a story of hereditary disaster—the suggestion, for instance, that no human act is ever an isolated thing, that evil inevitably breeds evil, that—in the words of Shelley paraphrasing a passage in Aeschylus—

> Revenge and wrong bring forth their kind,
> The foul cubs like their parents are;
> Their den is in the guilty mind
> And conscience feeds them with despair.

This fact of the hereditary curse on the house of Oedipus is brought home to the audience right at the beginning of the play, when Ismene is trying to dissuade Antigone from her enterprise; and it casts its shadow upon what is to come. 'Remember,' she says, 'how our father and mother died—and our brothers' . . .

> Now we two alone are left, and think what our doom will be
> If we flout the law and refuse to obey our king. . . .

But Antigone knows where her duty lies. 'Leave me my madness,' she answers; 'and let me suffer—a worse suffering would be to die ignobly.' That her determination is 'madness' she is well aware; for we misunderstand the play if we read it as some moderns do, as presenting a conflict between right and wrong, good and evil—the good being Antigone's love, the evil Creon's tyranny. It presents no such thing, but a much more deeply tragic conflict: the conflict, namely, not between right and wrong but between two rights. Antigone does not complain that her punishment is unjust; she knows, as a Greek audience would have known, that the law of the State, represented by Creon, must be upheld. Her punishment is cruel, but she recognizes it as inevitable. At the same time her rebellion is inevitable too, for had she not rebelled she would not have been Antigone. Creon's fault is not his punishing of Antigone, but the excessive and barbarous severity of his decree against the traitor Polynices—and it is that, which the prophet Teiresias tells him will bring him, too, to ruin. Antigone knows she must die, and she also knows that, though she is flouting the law of the State, she is obeying, as she cannot but obey, a higher law, the unwritten law of the human heart, derived mysteriously from God. When Creon asks her if she knew of his proclamation, 'Yes', she answers,

> But you are a man—no more—and no word of yours
> Can oversway God's law, unwritten, inalterable—
> Not made for time that passes, yesterday and today,
> But everliving and timeless, whose beginning no man knows.
> Not for fear of human pride would I break this law
> And be guilty before God.

I have said that the play presents the conflict between two rights; and so it does. But that is an inadequate way of describing its total effect. Its total effect cannot, indeed, be described at all; it can only be felt through submission to its poetry. It is the poetry which makes the reader, or spectator, aware that he—like the fabled persons of the old tale—is *in touch* with a mystery which thought cannot fathom, and linked with a destiny which is grander than he knew. Why do the passions of man inevitably destroy him, when at the same time they are what constitutes his glory? How is it that we know —as the chorus sings at the end of this play—that the 'crown of happiness is wisdom', yet find it so hard to be wise?

O love invincible, O conqueror,
You divide the spoils,
You set your night-watch in a girl's cheeks,
Over the sea you come against us, you shun not the shepherd's huts.
Neither god nor man can escape you, and your touch is madness.
You turn the heart of the just man to ill thoughts, to his ruin;
You have kindled the strife of son against sire;
The light of desire in a girl's eyes
Triumphs; established law yields to your rivalry
When you sit enthroned,
And Aphrodite laughs in joy of victory.

'Nothing too much'—everyone knows that old Greek proverb. To us, may be, it tastes a little flat; but then we live cooler lives than Sophocles and his contemporaries, and therefore have less need of such warning.

I have space to write of only two more of the plays, *Oedipus the King* and *Oedipus at Colonus*. Of the three

I pass over, *Electra* has some beautiful scenes but is, to my mind, somewhat statuesque and cold—like marble; *The Women of Trachis*, which is about the death of Heracles, I should like to write of, had I space, if only for the picture of the young wife, Deianira; *Philoctetes* I confess that I have never properly understood—that is, I do not care for it, except for the sound of the sea which echoes continually about the island of Lemnos, where Philoctetes is marooned, with his festering foot and his invincible bow. (Why, by the way, does Sophocles call Lemnos harbourless? He must have known; yet today it has a wonderful harbour, a huge circular lagoon, almost completely landlocked, with room for hundreds of large ships to ride in safety.)

Oedipus the King is the only play of Sophocles, or of any other Greek playwright, in which, apart from the poetry, the actual plot is a gripping one: or perhaps I should say the way the development of the plot is handled; for the final issue of the story, like that of all Greek plays, is of course foreknown. The legend, of which the play is concerned with a crucial incident, is as follows. Laius, King of Thebes, was told by an oracle of Apollo that he would have a son whose life would be accursed: it was his destiny to kill his father and marry his mother. The child was born. Was there any way to avert his appalling doom? Laius and his wife Jocasta thought that there was—the baby should be destroyed. Accordingly they gave it to a shepherd with orders that it should be exposed, with an iron pin through its ankles, in a lonely glen on Mt. Cithaeron, and left to die. But the shepherd's heart failed him, and he gave the child to another shepherd, a Corinthian, begging him to take it far away from Thebes and bring it up as his own. In time it was brought to Polybus, King of Corinth, who having no children adopted it, and gave it the name of Oedipus—Swollen-foot.

In the court of Polybus, Oedipus grew to manhood, believing himself the true son of his kind foster-parents. But one day, by chance or destiny, he came to hear of the fate which Apollo had foretold; so seeking, as Laius had sought, to escape from it, he ran away from Corinth, resolved never to return. In the course of his wanderings he came to Thebes—a city of which he knew nothing. There he found everything in confusion. Laius, the king, had just been killed by an unknown wayfarer; the Sphinx, a horrible monster, was devouring all who failed to answer her riddle. Oedipus answered it and thus destroyed the monster's power, and the Thebans in gratitude made him their king. All was then well with him—or so it seemed. He ascended the throne, and married the widowed queen, Jocasta.

For years—until his children were grown up—he lived in prosperity and happy ignorance, a wise ruler, honoured and beloved. But the Gods had not forgotten. Thebes was smitten with a plague, and the citizens once again looked to Oedipus to succour them.

At this point in the legend Sophocles' play begins. Oedipus has already sent his kinsman Creon to ask Apollo's oracle for guidance, and in the first scene of the play Creon returns with the 'good news' that all will be well once the unknown killer of Laius is discovered and either put to death or driven for ever, as a thing of pollution, from the city. Oedipus eagerly undertakes to find out the criminal.

There is no need for me to go on with the story. By a series of brilliantly-managed incidents and interlinked scraps of cumulative evidence we are made to watch first the vague dread, then the growing terror and finally the ghastly certainty in Oedipus' mind that the guilty man is himself: he it was who killed Laius at that chance encounter on the road; he it is who is now living as the husband of his mother. Only one end is possible for such a tale: Jocasta kills herself, and Oedipus, mad with horror, blinds himself with a pin from her dress, that he may never see again the once-loved things which by his guilt he has defiled—his house, his city, his people, and his children. Led by his daughter Antigone, he leaves Thebes for ever, an exile and a beggar.

This play, with the overtones and undertones of its dark poetry, has haunted the imagination of the world for more than two thousand years. I would not pretend to 'interpret' it, even in the limited way in which I tried to interpret *Ajax* and *Antigone.* The Greeks, as I have said, lived closer to death than we do; they were not cushioned as we are from the primitive things—from the hauntings, the menaces and mysteries, the irrational terrors, the darkness ever lying in wait. All their beautiful rationality and lucidity of thought, which we so justly admire, were only the sun-glitter on the surface of a sea of which the depths were unfathomable and filled with monsters. The play of *Oedipus* moves in these depths. What is human wisdom confronted with the vast Unknowable? Our seeming happiness is poised on a razor's edge (a favourite metaphor of Sophocles); there are things in the best of us which belong to the beast, and the home of one half of our nature is still, perhaps, the haunted wilderness—the wild mountain of Cithaeron, '*my* mountain', as Oedipus calls it, where his parents tried to kill him but failed. And the darkness is only deepened by the deliberately flat and conventional comment which Sophocles put into the mouth of the chorus at the close: *Call no man happy till he has died happy.*

There was a gap of many years between *Oedipus the King* and its sequel *Oedipus at Colonus,* which was almost certainly the last play that Sophocles wrote. The *Oedipus at Colonus* is a play of very great beauty, but I think it is not an easy one for a modern Englishman to understand without some knowledge of ancient Greek thought and feeling. Unlike the other plays I have described, it has little incident—little plot in the modern sense of the word. It is less like a play than a dramatic meditation on a theme—and the theme itself is a strange one, the sense, namely, that a man like Oedipus, who has suffered more than any man should be called upon to endure, and has, by Fate—or Chance (*Tyche* the 'way things happen')—offended against human law and the most sacred taboos, can yet, when his long life of anguish is over, bring a blessing to the place where he is buried. The curse which has destroyed him becomes a beneficent influence to the city—Athens—near which he lies. One is familiar with the idea of learning, or of purification, through suffering: it is to be found in Aeschylus, and in Keats, and in Shelley and in Shakespeare's *King Lear*; but the idea in this play is not quite that. Oedipus himself has learnt little: he is still a proud and passionate old man; he can still curse, with terrible effect as the course of the legend shows, his unfilial sons; he still looks upon himself as the sport of an incomprehensible and malignant Power. It is not he who has changed; he is the old Oedipus still; but he has become a man apart, a man upon whom the finger of a jealous god has been laid. He, the guiltless guilty one, has acquired a sort of sanctity, so that his ghost will have the power to bless.

The play opens with the arrival upon the stage of Oedipus and the faithful Antigone. In verse which has its own grave music Oedipus begins:

> Child of your old, blind father, tell me, Antigone,
> To what place have we come or to what city of men?
> Who today will welcome the vagrant with a scanty crust—
> Little I need, and with less than that little I am content;
> For three masters have taught me patience: grief and time—
> My long, long years—and a mind which is noble still.

Finding that they are at Colonus, near Athens, in a copse thick with laurel, olive and wild vine and filled with the song of nightingales—a grove which is sacred to the 'dread goddesses, daughters of Earth and Darkness, the all-seeing Kindly Ones'—Oedipus cries out that his destiny is fulfilled: his wanderings are over, for Apollo had foretold that when he came thither he would find rest at last. Such incidents as the play contains are provided by the attempt of Creon to get Oedipus to return to Thebes, his seizure of Antigone and her sister, their swift rescue by Theseus, the good king of Athens, and one very powerful scene in which Polynices comes from Thebes to back Creon's attempt, and is sent away by Oedipus with the curse which is afterwards fulfilled by his death—as we know from the *Antigone*. Theseus is persuaded to believe that the tomb of Oedipus will be a blessing to Athens, and at the end of the play, in response to the flash of lightning which is the promised sign from heaven, the blind beggar, suddenly erect and needing no guide, himself guides Theseus to the spot where he must die.

The play, like all Sophocles' plays, is haunted by Presences, but they are no longer malignant as they were in *Oedipus the King*. The dark gods are there still, but only, as it were, on the fringes of consciousness. The chorus can still say,

> Not to be born is best; but being born
> That man is luckiest who with all speed returns
> Thither, whence he came;

but the audience know better: they are brought to believe that such a negation is meaningless, and that human life, however bitter, yet has nobility and mystery because it is in touch with the unseen.

There is a device peculiar to Greek drama which I have not yet mentioned—the Messenger's speech. Partly for practical reasons, such as the nature of the stage and the scantiness of scenery and properties, partly for aesthetic reasons, Greek playwrights preferred scenes of violence—deaths, murders, suicides and so on—to happen off-stage and to be reported by a messenger. The suicide of Ajax, which takes place on the stage and is, indeed, the centre of the play, is exceptional. The device of the Messenger gave opportunities for imaginative description of a high order, and Sophocles took full advantage of them. The Messenger's account of the passing of Oedipus is perhaps the finest example of such speeches, and I quote it here—throwing over Sophocles' poetry 'the grey veil (to borrow Shelley's phrase) of my own words'.

> By the sheer chasm where the brazen steps lead down
> To the rock-roots in the dark, he chose one path
> Of the many that branch there, and near the basin in the rock

Where Theseus' covenant with Pirithous has its memorial,
He stopped, midway between it and the Thorician stone—
The hollow pear-tree and the marble tomb.
Then he sat down, and loosing his beggar's rags
Called to his children to bring running water to wash his body,
And for libation. And obedient to their father
They went quickly to the green knoll where stands Demeter's shrine,
And returned and washed him, and put the death-robe on him.

Then suddenly, when all was done as he desired,
The Lord of Darkness spoke in thunder; the girls
Shuddered at the voice, and fell weeping at their father's knees,
Lamenting and beating at their breasts for pity and fear.
And he at the sound of their crying
Took them in his arms, and said: 'This day, my children,
Is the end for me. All that was mine is gone, and never again
Will you labour, as you have long laboured, to care for me.
It was hard, I know; yet one word makes your labours light,
Love—the love you had from me as from no other.
But now we must part.'

So the three clung to one another, mingling their tears,
And when at last the passion of their weeping was stilled
There was silence—and in the silence the Voice
Of One who called to him, and the hair of their heads stood up for fear.
Again and yet again the God called: *Oedipus,*
Oedipus, why do we delay? You tarry too long.
And Oedipus, when he knew it was indeed God's voice,
Asked Theseus to come to him, and said: 'Promise me, friend,

Never to forsake my children, but to do for them
All that the wisdom of your heart prompts you'
And Theseus promised. Then Oedipus, laying on
his children his blind hands,
Said: 'You must be brave as becomes your blood, and go
Out of this place, not asking to witness the things
Which are not lawful for you to see or hear.
Go quickly; Theseus alone may know what is to be.'
Those words he spoke, and we all heard them, and
went away
With the two girls, weeping as they wept; and soon after
We looked back—and lo! Oedipus was gone—vanished
away.
Only Theseus we saw, his hand over his eyes
As if to screen them from some awful thing
He had seen, and could not bear to see.
And presently he made obeisance, saluting
The dark earth and the heaven in a single prayer.
He alone knows how Oedipus died—No fiery bolt
Killed him, no whirlwind from the sea rapt him away—
But God's messenger came for him, or the dark
underworld
Opened in love to receive him, without death's pain;
For his passing was not in anguish or grief, but
marvellous
Beyond all telling.

So ends this solemn and beautiful play, on which Sophocles lavished all the resources of his art—and in which, incidentally, he was able to give expression to his love for Colonus, where he was born—

white Colonus,
Earth's loveliest, where the nightingale's
Liquid notes most haunt
The darkness of green glades,
In her home amongst ivy dark as wine

And laurels thick with berries,
Holy with the presence of God, unpierced
By the sun and windless from the storms,
    Where Dionysus, the wild one, walks continually
    With the Nymphs who nursed him.

SHAKESPEARE

1564–1616

I WONDER if Shakespeare in those last few years of comfort and comparative affluence at New Place in Stratford-on-Avon, when with royal indifference he neglected to ensure the collection and publication of his plays, had any notion of how posterity would regard him. 'The best in this kind are but shadows . . .' Perhaps, had one asked him what he thought of his work, he might have replied that the plays were very well: they had served their purpose, given pleasure to gentle and simple, to the Court and the rag-tag of the London streets, and brought him money enough. Was not that sufficient reward for twenty years of gruelling labour, in the theatre and behind the scenes?

At that point, my imaginary questioner, seeing a half-smile on Shakespeare's lips and aware of a faint but pervading irony in the tone of his voice, might well have paused, though there was much more he would have liked to ask. I will pause too, as I know very well that fictions of this sort are likely to lead to absurdity. Nevertheless I begin with this fiction for a reason. The love felt for Shakespeare by most people in this country who know anything at all of literature, and the high place as playwright and poet accorded to him by educated people of every country in the world, are apt to obscure the fact that he was, in the first place, a practical craftsman and man of business. He knew his public and what his public wanted, and made no bones about providing it—never mind, at the moment, that he provided a great deal else besides. His public had an appetite for strong meat, and Shakespeare tossed it to them with a liberal hand—battles, murders, suicides, adulteries; mad lusts and madder revenges; minds crazed with grief, poisoned by ambition, alienated by disgust. Or, in other moods, he made them laugh, wooed them with fairy-tales and enchanted them with romance. It was all grand stuff; the playgoers devoured it and asked for more.

First, then, a practical craftsman: a sound man of business, determined to use his skills to earn a competence which would enable him one day to retire to his native town and to live respected there.

This fact that Shakespeare was primarily a practical craftsman, engaged in giving the playgoers what they wanted, suggests—to me, at any rate—a distinctive feature of his writing. Shakespeare's mature style is without artifice; he was a professional writer, but his style is the least professional of styles. It is unbookish. It seems as unconscious of its effect as the wind over a cornfield. If the burning coal had touched our lips, we should all, one feels, speak in Shakespeare's voice and with Shakespeare's accent. A poet by derivation means a maker, and many of the greatest poems declare themselves to be made things—like beautiful mosaics, the pieces artfully fitted, the colours artfully blended, all that is unassimilable set aside with delicate tact. Milton felt that an elephant's trunk and a hen were beneath the dignity of his Muse, who could not assimilate them; so the trunk became a lithe proboscis and the hen a tame villatic fowl. Shakespeare's poetry—and let me say at the outset that all Shakespeare's plays are also poems—has a different effect. It does not appear to have been made, but to have grown; and nothing comes amiss to it—even in its noblest passages the commonest objects are as much at home as a toad in the garden: Hamlet, begging his mother to admit her sin and repent, tells her not to spread compost on the weeds to make them ranker, and Antony to express his love for Cleopatra uses the image of a barge and its tow-rope. If the imagination has heat enough, there is nothing it cannot fuse.

Industrious scholars have told us that Shakespeare in the whole body of his work used some 24,000 different words. Milton, a copious writer, used about a third of that number. Now words correspond to things, and the fact that Shakespeare uses so many of them is another indication of the hospitality of his imagination, which shrank from nothing. All was grist to that mill. Bats, beetles, scabs, itch, mud, goats, buttons. . . . 'Ah yes,' I hear you say, 'there are plenty of scenes of common life in Shakespeare's plays, coarse, funny or farcical; and why should he not use such words?' My answer is that all those words, and fifty more no less homely and 'unpoetical', occur in passages of high and impassioned poetry, which they are fused with and miraculously exalt.

In itself this proves nothing; but, like the fact of Shakespeare's practical craftsmanship, it suggests a quality in him which is very important indeed: I mean the sheer scope and *quantity* of Shakespeare's concern with life and its circumstances. He liked to know, and did know, not only what people of all conditions suffered and enjoyed (his chief concern), but also what they did and how they did it. He was as familiar with Court etiquette as with the manners of the bawdy-house and the gutter; he got his technical terms always right, as in the sports of hunting, fencing, hawking, bowling, archery; the intricate language and practice of the law was an open book to him, and when he wrote of ships and the sea, as he did constantly, either directly or by way of allusion, he was invariably precise and accurate. Not Joshua Slocum himself could pick holes in the sheer technical perfection of the opening scene of *The Tempest*. The works of many good poets is like a walled garden, with *Trespassers will be Prosecuted* stuck on the gate; Shakespeare's work is a continent—with a hint of the oceans which wash its shores. 'Anyone,' Wordsworth remarked in an unfortunate moment, 'could write like Shakespeare if he had a mind to it,' to which Lamb, hitting the nail, as he generally did, on the head, replied: 'All that's lacking is, apparently, the mind.' Shakespeare took all knowledge for his province in a sense which Bacon, who claimed to do so, never did or could have done.

These are comparatively minor matters; but they have their interest, and help, I think, to explain Shakespeare's immediate success in his own day, as well as his continuing popularity with readers and playgoers of all grades of understanding. To understand Shakespeare 'to his depths', as Keats put it, is not the privilege of everyone, but any nitwit can enjoy him—and many do.

It is only natural that after Shakespeare had become famous stories should have been told about his youth, to take the place of biography. The known and established facts of his life are, however, extremely few. He was born in Stratford in April, 1564, the third child and eldest son of John Shakespeare, a prosperous tradesman, and sometime bailiff and alderman, of that town. His mother, Mary Arden, was the daughter of a wealthy neighbouring farmer. He was taught in the local Grammar School, which had a good reputation (this is an assumption only, but can be made with confidence). When he was eighteen he was married to Anne Hathaway, a woman eight years his senior. His first child, Susanna, was christened in Stratford parish church on May 26, 1583, his two other children, the twins Hamnet and Judith, on February 2, 1585. In 1592, when he was twenty-eight, we know from some spiteful remarks of a contemporary playwright, Robert Greene, that he was an actor in London and had already written plays—the three parts of *Henry VI*—for the company he was working with, Lord Strange's Men. In the two following years he published his two poems, *Venus and Adonis* and *The Rape of Lucrece*. In 1597 he bought the best house in Stratford, New Place, and settled there permanently in 1610. Business connected with his father's debts took him to Stratford frequently during the intervening years. In 1599 the Globe theatre was opened, on Bankside, and Shakespeare shared financially in the enterprise; he both acted, and wrote plays for the company, which was known as the Chamberlain's Men—afterwards, on the accession of James I, as the King's Men. Of the last sixteen years of his life, apart from records of his plays in the Stationer's Register and a few legal documents connected with the purchase of property in London and Stratford, no facts are known. His will survives. He died on April 23, 1616, at the age of fifty-two. His direct descendants were few: his daughter Judith had three sons who all died without children; his other daughter Susanna had one daughter who also died childless. Hamnet died before Shakespeare settled in New Place.

It is a meagre record. No less meagre are the personal references to him by contemporaries. His friends and fellow-actors Heminge and Condell, who did for us the inestimable service of collecting and publishing the plays in the famous First Folio of 1623, wrote in their preface to the volume that their object was 'onely to keepe the memory of so worthy a Friend and Fellow alive, as was our Shakespeare;' and another friend, Ben Jonson, in words which everyone knows, wrote: 'I loved the man, and do honour his memory on this side Idolatry, as much as any. He was indeed honest, and of an open and free nature.' John Aubrey, author of the *Brief Lives* and a tireless searcher after fact and anecdote, was told at second hand, some forty-five years after Shakespeare's death, that he was 'a handsome well-shaped man: very good company, and of a very ready and pleasant smooth wit.' The '*our* Shakespeare' of Heminge and Condell tells us a little; the warmth in Jonson's words a little more; Aubrey's 'handsome and well-shaped man' nothing whatever. I myself like to believe that Professor Dover Wilson is right in his guess that Shakespeare is the subject of the beautiful nameless portrait in the Rylands Library in Manchester—the portrait which he reproduces in his book *The Essential Shakespeare*.

One can play in fancy with the legends of deer-stealing, or of the penniless young husband holding horses' heads outside the theatres: but they are only legends. Of biographical facts we have almost none; of information about how he looked and spoke—again there is almost nothing. Does it matter? Not, perhaps, very much, though curiosity is a strong trait in most of us. (Keats said he would like to know 'in what position Shakespeare sat when he began "To be or not to be" ') Shakespeare's work has already been half-buried under libraries of comment and criticism, and it is just possible that if there were a full record of his life those literary men of today who turn even the washing-bills of the great to sinister purposes might have buried it deeper still. 'My spirit is thine,' Shakespeare wrote in a sonnet to his friend, 'the better part of me:' better, undoubtedly, than washing-bills, and it is there in his plays, not indeed to be explained, but for anyone to delight in if he cares to.

Shakespeare wrote poems before he wrote plays. When he moved on to play-writing, he was only one of a number of distinguished and successful contemporaries—Peele, Greene, Kyd, Marlowe, Chapman, then others a few years younger than himself, such as Dekker, Middleton, Marston, and the great Ben Jonson. Dramatics of some sort are in all countries amongst the most ancient and popular modes of amusement, but in England it was only during these latter years of Elizabeth I that the old mystery and morality plays were succeeded by a drama which could also rank as literature; but that drama remained popular in the best sense of the word. It had its affectations, stiffnesses, excesses; it paraded its learning and flaunted the banner of its rhetoric; but it depended upon popular support, and got it. The appetite for drama was avid, innocent and unspoiled, as was the appetite for life and knowledge, in proportion as the boundaries of both receded. The drama which fed that appetite was unsubtle and often violent; it did not, as in later ages, peep and pry into human motive; it did not question, or brood, or shrink, or titter. It was larger than life, hotter, fiercer and bloodier: Marlowe's Barabas and Tamburlaine are monsters, if you will; but determined as they are to drink life to the lees and damn the consequences, they were able to cast a strong spell over the imaginations of men who under the stimulus and excitement of the discovery of new lands in the west by the enterprise of English seamen, and the growing sense of national unity and strength were coming more and more to take the world as their oyster. Moreover, the drama of the day had found for itself the mighty auxiliary of poetry.

Shakespeare, then, had the form ready to his hand. Naturally, he took it. It was good business to take it; and also (we may surmise) he saw in it a vehicle of boundless potentialities. Poetic drama is the summit and crown of poetry; for us, wise after the event, it is easy to say this: Shakespeare, one guesses, saw—like Lady Macbeth, in a somewhat different context—the future in the instant.

Nevertheless Shakespeare, like everyone else, had to learn his craft. His earliest plays, except in flashes, are not distinguishable in quality from those of his contemporaries. He also had to live and suffer—for Milton was right when he said that a good book was the precious life-blood of a master spirit, and men are not apt to be master spirits at the age of twenty-eight.

No generalization about Shakespeare can be more than a quarter true: attempt one, and he confounds you. None the less, here are three: as a dramatist Shakespeare, as he grew in power, passed from the dramatic representation of *themes* (*Richard II*, for example, is about the nature of kinghood, *Romeo and Juliet* is about young lovers crossed in love, *The Taming of the Shrew* is about—well—the taming of a shrew) to the creation of characters: i.e. to the presentation in the round of individual men and women who, because of their intensely realized individuality, are for that very reason the vehicle for 'themes' of far subtler, deeper and more universal significance. One human heart is, or can be, a microcosm of a world's anguish and delight. Secondly, as a poet—as a man, that is, whose work is a reflection of his experience—Shakespeare passed from gaiety to near despair, and thence, towards the end of his life, to a temper of mind half humorous, half ironic yet wholly tender, in which with infinite understanding and indulgence he could watch the goings-on of men and women in this wicked but enchanting world, secure—it may be—in the knowledge that the coloured and moving pageant is only the shadow of a reality beyond our grasp. Not only are the best *in this kind* but shadows; we ourselves, too, are such stuff as dreams are made on.

Thirdly, Shakespeare progressively modified and finally brought to a beauty and subtlety unsurpassed in English poetry the blank verse line which he took over from his contemporaries and predecessors. Marlowe had done great things with it already: his verse is as proud as a banner 'flouting the sky' and fans us into admiration. Shakespeare's verse does something different, which I will not try to describe; but read again the well-known lines in *Dr. Faustus*:

> Is this the face that launched a thousand ships
> And burned the topless towers of Ilium.
> Sweet Helen make me immortal with a kiss....

and then, while the music of them is still in your ears, follow it with:

> Unarm, Eros; the long day's task is done
> And we must sleep.

or:

> when you sing,
> I'd have you buy and sell so; so give alms;
> Pray so, and for the ordering your affairs
> To sing them too. When you do dance, I wish you
> A wave o' the sea, that you might ever do
> Nothing but that...

Pedantries about caesuras and pauses and end-stopped lines may be all very well, but they hardly seem to the purpose. To chatter of such things in an attempt to explain the movement of Shakespeare's verse is like trying to explain the beauty of a face by an inventory of the features—'item: two lips, indifferent red ...' The movement must be felt and the music heard by the ear and the *inward* ear; and anyone who cannot hear it must be very deaf indeed.

I have made my three generalizations simply for convenience: actually, they are all part of a single process, the development, namely, of the true Shakespearian drama, which is the drama of character—the drama in which the plot is important only because of the people who are involved in it. In the early plays the signs begin to appear in one or two minor, and mostly comic, figures: Don Armado, for instance, in *Love's Labour's Lost* (1594) Speed and Launce in *Two Gentlemen of Verona* (1593). These at least begin—to borrow Logan Pearsall Smith's phrase—to talk themselves alive. With

Romeo and Juliet (1595) there is a leap forward with the Nurse and Mercutio, both minor figures. In *Richard II* (1595) for all its beauty, no-one, to my ear, talks himself alive except, perhaps, the gardeners, and certainly no-one in *A Midsummer Night's Dream* (1596) except Bottom and his friends. This is not an adverse criticism of these plays—nobody needs to be told that the last three of them are enough to have made any poet immortal; I make the point only to indicate that they are no more than a foreshadowing of what Shakespeare was a few years later to do. Had he died after writing the *Dream*, we should hardly remember him as a playwright at all, but only as a poet—perhaps our best, though run very close by half a dozen others—who elected to write dramatic poetry, interspersed with prose scenes of a highly idiosyncratic, and indeed tantalizing, flavour, which made us wonder a little peevishly why we were offered so tasty a dish only to have it snatched away. 'No, 'tis not so deep as a well, nor so wide as a church door; but 'tis enough, 't will serve. Ask for me tomorrow, and you shall find me a grave man. . . . A plague on both your houses!' What, we might say, is this fellow Mercutio up to, mocking the lunar and dreamlike radiance of a poem of young love? The answer would be that Shakespeare's daemon was beginning to work, whether he wished it or not.

The daemon finally got loose two years later with *The Merchant of Venice*; it wrecked the play—or made it: which, depends upon one's feelings about the parts of the play in which Shylock is not concerned. Personally, I can read the play only for Shylock's sake, as I find the casketry tedious and turn cold when Portia lectures us on the quality of mercy without the least intention of practising it herself. But Shylock is a miracle: he is the first character to take on fully that *independent* life which is the mark of all Shakespeare's great figures. I use the words 'daemon' and 'miracle' advisedly; for the creation of Shylock does seem to have occurred in some odd way against Shakespeare's conscious will. Shakespeare cared little for the shapeliness of his plots and nothing for their verisimilitude; but he cared a great deal for their unity of tone and colour and this unity Shylock disrupts. That tragic figure of flesh and blood is utterly at odds with the muted and fairytale world of love-making at Belmont. It is more than likely that, Jew-baiting being then, as at other times, a popular sport, Shakespeare first thought of him as a figure of fun. Then the thing happened: Shylock grew under his hand as he wrote, expanded into humanity under the warmth of his compassionate imagination. Hath not a Jew eyes. . . ? indeed he has.

Shakespeare, when he created Shylock, had begun his true work. The path, though still 'through forth-rights and meanders', into a new country for the drama and for English literature, already beckoned him on. He had finished with dramatic poetry and was embarked, once and for all, upon the wide ocean of poetic drama. In the former, the stage-play had been only, as it were, an excuse for the poetry—or, say, the dish to serve it up in; in the latter the poetry is an integral part—more, it is the very soul of the drama itself. And concurrently with the development of this new function of his poetry, Shakespeare was perfecting a brilliant and subtle prose, which he was to use with ever increasing effect, especially in comedy.

Some scientists, following the Abbé Lemaître, have

supposed that the universe was once contained, pressed small, in the Primeval Atom. The Atom exploded into the universe as we know it now. It sounds, indeed, rather like one of Blake's Memorable Fancies, but it will serve as an image for what seems to have happened to Shakespeare's creative genius at, or immediately after, the time when he wrote *The Merchant of Venice*. During the next three years, till the end of the crucial year 1600, Shakespeare's greatest comic characters were created: Sir Toby Belch, Malvolio and, above all, Falstaff. Unlike their predecessors in the early plays, these three dominate the plays in which they occur. It was an astonishing period: the two parts of *Henry IV*, *As You Like It*, *Henry V* and *Twelfth Night* were written in rapid succession.

Up to 1600, then, Shakespeare's presiding spirit was the spirit of comedy. Apart from Shylock, apart from the panache and swashbuckling rhetoric of the Histories —Hotspur, in *Henry IV*, is the only non-comic character who really 'talks himself alive'—apart from *Romeo and Juliet* of which I shall say something later, all his triumphs had been in comedy. Now Shakespearian comedy is a complex thing, and needs a word or two of comment. It seems to me that the two finest comedies—*As You Like It* and *Twelfth Night*—are, in their way, as much a reading of life as any other sort of play, tragedy included. One is inclined to associate only lightheartedness and jokes with the word 'comedy': in Shakespeare's comedy there is, indeed, plenty of both, but they are nevertheless only strands in the tapestry. It is fashionable nowadays to suppose that the tragic view of life is the only profound and 'true' one. Modern playwrights who wish to be taken seriously compete with one another in frustration and despair, as if it were indecent to enjoy one's dinner or take pleasure in a kiss. But this is all too simple a view of things, and springs, I fancy, from a failure of vitality. Shakespeare was less invertebrate—or knew better. I could not without absurd inadequacy describe in a sentence the effect of *Twelfth Night*; but I do know that it persuades me afresh of the truth of Blake's saying that

> Joy and grief are woven fine,
> A garment for the soul divine,

even though grief is absent from this play. None the less it could not have been written by a man ignorant of the dark shadow which gives a poignancy to gaiety. Only the wise can play the fool to good effect, and the laughter of the wise is like the shimmer on the surface of the sea. How delicately in this wonderful play Shakespeare keeps the balance between the dream and the waking world, making the one mock the other and uniting the two in the person of Viola, who is equally at home in both—and with what tact he draws back from the edge of cruelty in the discomfiture of Malvolio. The interplay between self-deception ('if music be the food of love, play on') and actuality ('a plague o' these pickled herring!') each throwing cross-lights on the other and repeated in varied patterns in every character in the play, is an image of the human mind itself, which, however much we pretend that it is concerned only with a mysterious something called reality, yet builds up its totality of experience with just such a kaleidoscope of lights and half-lights, always in doubt of the precise dividing line between twilight and day. With ever so small a shift of emphasis the dream, which in Shakespeare's golden comedies is a happy one, may turn to nightmare or to horror. There is a passage in Plato where Socrates and Aristophanes are represented as discussing the question whether the same man should be capable of writing both tragedy and comedy. The course the discussion took is not reported but we, at any rate, know the answer. Shakespeare has shown us that comedy—*his* comedy—and tragedy may represent, like Blake's Songs of Innocence and Songs of Experience, the 'two contrary states' of a human soul. In Shakespeare the one, as was proper, preceded the other in dominance; but both were there, co-existing, from the first, and they were ultimately to be resolved and reconciled. *Twelfth Night* is haunted by music—and all the music is melancholy. It begins with music, a strain with a 'dying fall', and it ends with music which, to my ear (though I do not know the tune and can hear only the words) is more melancholy still, with a sadness more piercing and more innocent even than *Come away death.* That melancholy is surely one strand in the rich tapestry of this play, and to us, at any rate, with our advantage in time, it sounds like a warning of what was to come.

Twelfth Night has been justly called Shakespeare's 'farewell to mirth'. After it he wrote no more comedies: to be sure, he wrote one or two plays which he *called* comedies, but in them the old sweetness ('sweet' is one of Shakespeare's favourite words) had turned sour. The period from 1601 to 1607 was the period of the tragedies.

All writing of any worth, whatever its form, is, I suppose, in the last analysis, personal. A man can write only of what he knows—perhaps only of what he *is*, though he may find a thousand shapes in which to embody it. 'Shakespeare,' Keats said, 'led a life of allegory; his works are a comment on it.' People have speculated and will continue to speculate upon what it was, either in his intimate life or in external events, that caused the change at this time in the whole colour and temper of his work. His sonnets (not to be dated exactly) hint at a story of personal disillusionment, and no doubt he was deeply affected by the disgrace of his friend and first patron the Earl of Southampton, who was involved in the treason of the Earl of Essex. Essex had been an admired popular figure, the 'glass of fashion and the mould of form', and his sudden downfall and death came to the country as a whole like the inexplicable putting-out of a familiar light, while the end of the reign, coming soon after, and the accession of James I with his ignoble court and more ignoble policy must have seemed to one of Shakespeare's temper the end of an epoch indeed. But all such speculations are idle, and it is better simply to observe the fact: I would put it like this, that, whereas in the earlier plays Shakespeare was aware (as who isn't?) of *evils*, in the succeeding tragedies he was aware, and overwhelmingly, of *evil*. The shift of emphasis had occurred, and the dream had turned to nightmare. Lack-love, treachery, treason, hatred, sensuality, greed—there is not one of the vices which make us men that is not present in the early Histories and Comedies; but they are chained monsters. In the tragedies Evil itself, a palpable Presence, has burst its bonds and roams the world, challenging the noblest to mortal combat and allowing them to prove their grandeur only in their defeat. It is fitting that *Hamlet* the first of the great tragedies—*Julius Caesar* was the false dawn, like that which seamen know, preceding the true—should be a tragedy of disillusionment. The young Prince, brilliant, happy, loving and beloved, suddenly finds by his father's death, the discovery of its cause, and his mother's subsequent betrayal, that the bottom has fallen out of his world. The smear of a slug's trail is over everything he once saw as beautiful, especially over his love for Ophelia, and he is forced furiously to re-think all his values, to find his way in a universe where black and white seem to have changed places. No wonder his will to act is paralysed; no wonder he tells his lover to hide herself in a nunnery, where alone she may keep herself clean from the 'nasty stye'; no wonder he clings to Horatio, decent and ordinary, with no imagination to turn corrupt, as a drowning man clutches at a straw.

Writers on Shakespeare are often taken to task for interpreting as personal statements of Shakespeare's own what he puts into the mouths of his characters, as if they forgot that he was writing *plays*. It is possible, no doubt, to be very foolish in this matter—as by the assertion, for instance, that Shakespeare thought life was like a tale told by an idiot, because he makes Macbeth say so. But it is essential at the same time to remember that each play in its entirety, in its total imaginative effect, is a personal statement of the most profound and comprehensive kind. Now in *Hamlet* one element, and a very powerful one, in the complex statement is revulsion and disgust, following (as always) upon disillusionment; and the same revulsion and disgust recur with increasing emphasis in play after play —in *Othello* which is a story of sexual jealousy, a theme Shakespeare treated in no less than four plays; again, with an almost frightful pervasiveness, in *King Lear*, where in addition to the double theme of the betrayal of parents by children and the presence of Regan, beside whom even Iago seems to have some natural humanity, the lunatic and semi-lunatic ravings of the King image the whole world of the heart's experience as a hollow sham of hypocrisy and lust; and again in *Timon of Athens*, where the cold sanity of Timon's hatred and condemnation of his fellowmen is more dreadful even than Lear's madness. In *Timon* the sense of revulsion and disgust is not merely all-pervasive, but overwhelming.

What had happened to 'sweetest Shakespeare, Fancy's child'? Never mind what had happened, but, having noted the fact, let us note another fact, which is much more astonishing: namely that with the exception of *Timon* all these plays, *Hamlet*, *Othello*, *Lear* and *Macbeth* (in which last revulsion and disgust have disappeared, to be succeeded by a sort of cosmic darkness and horror) leave us, the spectators or readers, not crushed or annihilated as one might suppose, not with a sense of embitterment or despair, but with a knowledge, never before so sure, of the nobility of the human spirit and the greatness of the destiny of man. That this should be so is one of the inexplicable mysteries of Shakespeare's art.

Nevertheless, inexplicable though it is in any final sense, as all the great absolutes by which we live—divinity, *reality*, beauty, love—are inexplicable, we can, and must, go a little way towards understanding it. Here, then, are a few pointers. Shakespeare's tragedies, like his comedies, are a reading of life: a deeper reading, not because the tragic view is necessarily truer than any other, but because Shakespeare himself was more deeply involved in them. The writer of comedies stands a little aloof: he is a spectator, affectionate, amused, cynical—whatever it may be, of the goings-on of men; the writer of tragedy enters the arena, and does battle. I think the first thing to notice about Shakespeare's tragedies is that they all in one sense end happily. They tell the story of a struggle—'good' people against 'bad' people—and the good people win. In *Hamlet*, when all the agonies are over and the king and queen have met the fate they deserved, the sun comes out again over Denmark with the promise of a comfortable future under Fortinbras, the 'delicate and tender prince'; in *Othello* the excellent and honourable Cassio succeeds to the government of Cyprus; in *Lear* the wicked party —the unnatural son, the unnatural daughters and all their minions—is defeated, and Albany (a much improved character) the noble Kent and the virtuous Edgar find themselves in control of England's destinies; in *Macbeth*, the bloody tyrant at last goes down, and Birnam wood comes to Dunsinane bringing dawn at last after the long and dreadful uncertainties of the night. In short, life goes on; the normal, the decent, the unspectacular, all of which are necessary to the continuity of life, triumph; they conquer their opposites, but—and this is the point—at what a cost! The victory can come only, it seems, by the destruction not simply of the forces of disruption and evil but also of those very qualities which, on a partial view, are the most precious of all. The finest spirits are doomed by the very nature of things to be destroyed. What life loses and is bound to lose in its impersonal and relentless course is precisely that which gives it nobility—its own best part. Hamlet must die as well as Claudius, Cordelia as well as Regan.

Such appears to be the general, large-scale pattern of

Shakespeare's tragedies; and there is a similar pattern in the individual lives of his principal characters. In them, as persons, a similar conflict is fought out: similar, but not the same, for in them the conflict is not between 'good' and 'bad', but between diverse elements in themselves and circumstances for which they are in part responsible and which ensure—life being what it is—that their defeat shall come as a consequence not, by any means, only of their weakness, but often of their finest qualities. It was *because* Hamlet was a better man than most, with a more vivid and impassioned sense of men's honour and of women's purity, that he was forced to play a part that destroyed him; the gullibility of Othello was the direct consequence of the noblest part of his nature, the ability to give his heart away with utter confidence and trust; it was the exalted political idealism of Brutus that made him no match for the worldly and capable Antony; even Macbeth's destruction sprang, at least in part, from what there was of finer essence in that hag-ridden and haunted breast—the communication with the unseen world and with what lies behind appearances, which he shares with poets. Life, it would seem, has no use for excesses; its business is to continue itself; and for that purpose it most favours the norm: Horatio is life's darling, not Hamlet; Edgar and Albany, not Lear. Nevertheless, realizing this, we realize at the same time that what life rejects is precisely that which makes it most worth living. That is the tragedy. It is also the reason for our exultation, for we know, seeing or reading these plays, that without the splendour and nobility of these passions of the human heart, however self-destructive they may be, life would be mean and poor.

These ideas about the nature of life which I have tried to formulate are never directly expressed in the plays; indeed, it is not the function of any art to express ideas about life directly. But the difference between true and false art is that the 'meaning' of the former is never circumscribed, however precise its apparent subject may be. It dwells in the mind and ferments there. There is no such thing as an isolated object or an isolated thought; between all there runs an invisible connecting thread, and the mystery of art is that, by intensely imagining—that is, by entering into the innermost truth of—a particular thing or person the artist thereby reveals its connections with a million others. It is because Hamlet, for instance, is so intensely individualized, because he is precisely himself and no-one else down to the smallest tricks of speech ('very like, very like . . .' 'except my life, except my life, except my life.') that we all see in him a part of our own hearts. 'Many men,' said Edward Thomas, the poet, 'have thought that *Hamlet* was written for them: I *know* that it was written for me.'

I have said something about the effect of these tragedies, and the means to that effect is the creation of character. The great comedies were comedies of character; the great tragedies are in a supreme degree tragedies of character. This is the reason why *Romeo and Juliet* is not a tragedy in the proper Shakespearian sense. It is not a tragedy because the deaths of the lovers are not a necessary consequence of what they *are*: their deaths depend upon a letter which went astray—an *accident*. An accident may be touching or terrible, but it is not tragedy. Romeo's death could not be a result of what he *was*, because Shakespeare gave him no character at all—and not much to Juliet. They are two young lovers, and nothing more. This exquisite play is not, in fact, drama at all, as Shakespeare afterwards taught us to understand the word: it is a love-poem, cast in dramatic form. When Shakespeare wrote it he was indeed a poet, but by no means of the sort that he was later to become.

If the means to the effect of the great tragedies is the creation of character, the means to the creation of character is poetry. A poet always, Shakespeare was a supreme poet only in these later plays. Prose in all the tragedies, he continues to use, and with increasing subtlety and effect: often it is a deliberate foil to the poetry, used in scenes of lower emotional pitch; by bumpkins and scallywags; or by leading characters in scenes subsidiary to the main theme, as when Hamlet talks to the players; by Iago constantly, making us feel the hateful reality of that vile, cold mind; by the porter in *Macbeth*, to give us a breathing-space, though a short one and none too pleasant, between two scenes of almost unbearable tension; and once, for a different purpose, in the marvellous scene of Lady Macbeth's sleep-walking. But the soul of all the plays is in the poetry—once, the play had been merely the framework of the poetry; now the poetry is the very stuff of the drama itself. I do not know what poetry is, and its ultimate mystery, like the mystery of life, must remain dark; but I do know that when Cleopatra says,

> No more but e'en a woman, and commanded
> By such poor passion as the maid that milks
> And does the meanest chares

she is then revealed in all her royalty; I know that I do not understand the depth of Lear's anguish until he says to Cordelia,

Come, let's away to prison:
We two alone will sing like birds i' the cage;
When thou dost ask me blessing, I'll kneel down
And ask of thee forgiveness . . . ;

or the quality of Othello's love for Desdemona before he whispers,

Put out the light and then—put out the light.

I know too that it is the poetry in *Macbeth* which links the darkness in the mind of the murderer and his fiend-like queen with another darkness, impalpable and pervasive and akin to their own:

There's husbandry in heaven:
Their candles are all out.

And with what power, when the Sergeant at the opening of the play describes the rebels killed by Macbeth in honourable battle as 'strange images of death', does the grim phrase cast its glare forward upon the more awful images of his murdered men. Shakespeare's language is often compressed, tortured, difficult; but no-one who cares for his poetry can have failed to wonder at the tact which enables him again and again in moments of high emotional tension in the plays to use a speech so devoid of the trappings of poetry, so pure and transparent that one is hardly conscious of words at all:

I kissed thee ere I killed thee . . .

I shall find time, Cassius; I shall find time . . .

Pray you, undo this button. . . .

> Peace, peace!
> Dost thou not see my baby at my breast
> That sucks the nurse asleep?

or when in Hamlet love for an instant gets the better of horror and rage, and to his mother's cry that he has cleft her heart in twain, he answers:

> O throw away the worser part of it
> And live the purer with the other half.

These things are crown of poetry, and at the same time the inmost pulse of the drama.

King Lear and *Macbeth* were both written in 1606—a good year's work. In 1607 Shakespeare wrote his last two tragedies, *Antony and Cleopatra* and *Coriolanus. Antony and Cleopatra* is for me the one play of all his plays that I could least spare. In it Shakespeare is at the summit of his powers and seems to have attained a new and sovereign ease and mastery—not over his material only but over the life within himself. The anguish has gone. 'Classical' is the last word one would apply to Shakespeare, yet in this play—'coloured with magnificence'—there is a touch of the classical detachment. Shakespeare, one feels, is no longer *involved*, as he was involved in *Hamlet, Othello* and *Lear*. The play reminds one of Keats' image of poetry as

> might half slumbering on his own right arm.

It is Shakespearian tragedy in the full sense which I have tried to describe, but this time it leaves no tears or pain for the inevitable waste in the struggle with evil of what is delicate, or fine, or true, but only gratitude, and a kind of awe at the strangeness and the incalculable

Mansell Collection

SOPHOCLES

Bust in the Capitoline Museum, Rome

Mansell Collection

SHAKESPEARE

The Droeshout portrait, from the First Folio

grandeurs of human destiny. And this Shakespeare achieves through the story of a minx and a libertine—as they might appear to other eyes, and did appear to Philo, who makes it very plain in the opening words of the play. This is one measure of Shakespeare's greatness: he never cheated; he never invented characters to suit a theme, or fashioned a monster—virtuous or otherwise—to play the part of a man. As with Antony and his queen, so it was with Falstaff: Shakespeare imagined a fat, gross man, a bolting-hutch of beastliness, a roast Manningtree ox with a pudding in his belly, a coward, a wastrel, a liar of ineffable resource—and proceeded to make us love him; and love him we do, and still weep, as I am sure Shakespeare's own audiences wept, with a sense of irreparable loss when Mistress Quickly tells, in *Henry V*, how she watched him die in his bed.

Antony and Cleopatra was followed in the same year by *Coriolanus*, about which I shall say nothing except that when Shakespeare wrote it the molten metal of his imagination seems to have cooled. It is a noble play, but hard and craggy, and does not take us—if the expression is intelligible—beyond itself, as the greatest plays do. The highest poetry creates a kind of light by which we see, or have glimpses of, other things than the immediate subject of it. I think that this light is absent from *Coriolanus*.

I said on a previous page that the two 'contrary states', as represented by Shakespeare's comedies on the one hand and by his tragedies on the other, were to be finally reconciled. The reconciliation now came, and the outcome of it was two great plays, *Cymbeline* (Tennyson's favourite of all) and *The Winter's Tale*—and one supreme one, *The Tempest*. A number of writers on Shakespeare have used the word 'reconciliation', to describe the last change which came over his work; it is a useful word, not, perhaps, altogether satisfactory, because in an important sense the reconciliation had already been effected in the tragedies, especially in *King Lear*. Indeed it is precisely in that fact that its greatness lies: it is incomparably the most terrible of the plays; it contains, so to speak, a wider area of anguish and a blacker abyss of disillusionment, hatred and bitterness than any other; but the whole point and effect of the play, as a work of art and a reading of human life, is that Lear had necessarily, by the very constitution of things, to endure his hell in order to reach his heaven. And he does reach it; the gods do give the poor passionate old man the 'patience' he prays for; the knowledge, so cruelly won, of Cordelia's affection, though it cannot obliterate does indeed 'redeem' all sorrows that ever he has felt. When he is dying, and Edgar tries to call his spirit back, Kent, who is wiser, says No:

> he hates him,
> Who would upon the rack of this tough world
> Stretch him out longer.

This world has done its worst with him, but no-one who knows the play as it should be known can feel that this is the end. Lear has found his truth and—to borrow Keats' phrase—dies into life. 'The excellence of every art,' Keats wrote, 'is its intensity capable of making all disagreeables evaporate from their being in close relationship with Beauty and Truth.' No man was ever less of a 'pessimist' than Shakespeare; the pessimist believes that human life is empty and meaningless, or the sport of an ironic God; Shakespeare, aware as no-one was ever aware of inevitable suffering and waste, at the same time saw always at the heart of life an inextinguishable radiance, which bestiality and greed and folly and hatred could never wholly obscure. Therein is his triumph. At one moment he lost that vision—when he wrote *Timon of Athens*, and that is the reason why the play is a failure.

The vision was reached, or maintained, in the great tragedies only through struggle; in them we are witnesses of the struggle, its expense of spirit and its pain. Suddenly it ceased. Everyone knows how after a period of physical pain one is flooded, when it stops, with an almost unimaginable sense of relaxation, of ease, of gratitude. That will serve as a poor metaphor for what seems to have happened to Shakespeare's spirit after he had written *Coriolanus* and had returned, at least for long periods, to Stratford. The change is reflected in his last three plays, especially in the last of all, *The Tempest*.

I have not space to say more than a word about these plays. The first two, *Cymbeline* and *The Winter's Tale*, beautiful though they are, are only preparatory to the final triumph of *The Tempest*. I call *The Tempest* a triumph not only in a laudatory sense, but because it does actually represent a triumph of Shakespeare's spirit. With it, Shakespeare has emerged once for all from the Valley of the Shadow. Evil has lost its power over him; no less aware of it than before, he can now confront it without a shudder, almost with a smile. He has come to 'see as a god sees'—I find myself constantly quoting Keats, and not without reason, for apart from the fact there was a real kinship of spirit between him and Shakespeare, the best criticism of Shakespeare is to be found in casual utterances scattered about in Keats' letters. It is tempting, and too easy, to 'philosophise' *The Tempest*, and thus ruin it as a supreme poetic drama. But what actually happens in the play? A Duke, less interested in governing his dukedom than in gaining knowledge, is seized by his treacherous brother and his confederates, shoved into a boat with his baby daughter, and abandoned to almost certain death. The boat, miraculously, brings them in safety to an island. Here the Duke by continued study and thought masters all human and superhuman knowledge. The elements obey him, spirits are at his command. By means of the power this knowledge gives him, he brings his enemies, helpless, to the island—and forgives them. The final impulse to forgive comes from his spirit of spirits, Ariel, who riding like poetry itself on the curled clouds, or doing business in the veins of the earth, or fetching dew at midnight from the still-vexed Bermoothes, has always been faithful to his behests.

> The rarer action is
> In virtue than in vengeance....

and it was Ariel who taught him this—Taught whom? Prospero—or Shakespeare? It matters little. But the forgiveness comes, with a smile, perhaps, half tender half ironic for all the bustle and struggle and ferment of life in this bewildering world, which itself, like the cloud-palaces in the sky, is destined to dissolve, leaving 'not a wrack behind.' I always remember with gratitude some words of Sir Arthur Quiller-Couch on *The Tempest*, and I cannot do better than quote them here: in seeing or reading this play, 'we feel,' he wrote, 'that we are greater than we know. So on the surge of our emotion, as on the surges ringing Prospero's island, is blown a spray, a mist. Actually it dwells in our eyes, bedimming them: and as involuntarily we would brush it away, there rides in it a rainbow; and its colours are wisdom and charity, with forgiveness, tender ruth for all men and women growing older, and perennial trust in young love.'

If we wanted one reason out of a thousand for loving Shakespeare, we might well do worse than choose this miracle, that he who of all men sounded most deeply the abyss of human anguish and despair was able in the end to imagine a Miranda.

> How beauteous mankind is! Oh brave new world
> That has such people in 't!

And with a royal charity he allows us to believe that for her, at least, it will never crumble into a 'quintessence of dust'. Though she never, even in Naples, learned the irrepressible gaiety and wit of Rosalind, she continued, we assure ourselves, to love her Ferdinand, and when she came, as all men and women must, to hear the 'still, sad music of humanity', she listened to it with the understanding of a heart which had never lost its innocence.

I have touched only the fringes of my subject. Anyone, I fancy, who sits down to write a few pages of general comment upon Shakespeare must feel like the young Indian student who was faced with an examination paper containing a single question only: *Write everything you know*. Let us hope that the poor young man knew nothing, for that would have facilitated selection. I should have liked, for instance, if space had allowed me, to say more of the women in Shakespeare's plays; for in his representation of women and of their relationship with men Shakespeare—apart from the intrinsic truth and wholesomeness of his vision—was a thousand miles ahead of his age. Always in his plays women are, for good or evil, the spiritual and emotional equals of men. I have read that the first English poet to connect love and marriage was Spenser, Shakespeare's elder contemporary, in *The Faërie Queene*: not much knowledge of Shakespeare is needed to know that the connection was as natural to his mind as was breathing to his body. The cross-currents between men and women have always been, for one mood, a subject for laughter, and there is in Shakespeare's early plays plenty of badinage on the subject and still more innuendo—often so subtle that it must have set a problem to Dr. Bowdler; but whenever a true love-relationship is central in a play, Shakespeare handles it, in his comedies, with a freshness, gaiety and balance, and in his tragedies with a masculine directness and strength very far removed from the impotent and tortured analysis of much modern writing.

Another note:— it has often been said that Shakespeare never judged: that, unlike lesser writers, he had no moral axe to grind. Up to a point this is true: certainly he ground no axe, being far too much of a poet and artist to do any such thing. He had an unprecedented breadth of sympathy and knowledge of men (Coleridge called him the 'myriad-minded Shakespeare') and could project himself into characters of the most diverse kinds, including the angelic and the monstrous. But to say that he never judged is, I think, to go too far—and no compliment to Shakespeare. Nothing is more evident from familiarity with his plays than the qualities in human character which he detested and despised. It would be tedious to make a list of them here, but I will mention one: hypocrisy. In the savage denunciations of Timon and in the ravings of Lear hypocrisy, in one form or another, is the central theme; and it may be worth while to notice that Falstaff and Autolycus, the two splendid scoundrels whom we love because Shakespeare loved them, never pretended to be other than they were. They were both entirely honest rogues. Anything which smelt even slightly of sanctimoniousness was to Shakespeare anathema.

Finally: Shakespeare was a playwright and a consummate master of his craft. If in what I have written I have paid more attention to his poetry than to his dramatic expertise I have done it deliberately; for the plays to be properly enjoyed must be read as well as seen upon the stage. I suppose this is true of all great plays by any author; but it is pre-eminently true of Shakespeare, whose prodigality of invention was like what Cleopatra said of Antony's pleasures:

> his delights
> Were dolphin-like; they showed his back above
> The element they lived in.

Lamb, who was amongst the most sensitive critics of Shakespeare, thought that *King Lear* ought not to be acted at all. Few would agree with this judgement. Shakespeare wrote it to be acted, and acted it should be; nevertheless it, like the other tragedies and like all the plays in a lesser degree, yields its full meaning only gradually and only to patient study.

The order and dating of Shakespeare's plays have

been determined only comparatively recently—even now the precise dating is often doubtful. I append a chronological list, which I have taken in part from F. E. Halliday's book, *Shakespeare and his Critics*.

Approximate chronological list of the Plays

1590	Henry VI, Part 2
	Henry VI, Part 3
1591	Henry VI, Part I
1592	Richard III
1593	Comedy of Errors
1594	Love's Labour's Lost
1595	Romeo and Juliet
	Richard II
1596	The Taming of the Shrew
	A Midsummer Night's Dream
1597	King John
	Merchant of Venice
	Henry IV, Part 1
1598	Henry IV, Part 2
	Merry Wives of Windsor
1599	Henry V
	Much Ado About Nothing
1600	As You Like It
	Twelfth Night
1601	Julius Caesar
	Hamlet
1602	Troilus and Cressida
1603	All's Well that Ends Well
	Measure for Measure
1604	Othello
1605	Timon of Athens
1606	King Lear
	Macbeth

1607	Antony and Cleopatra
	Coriolanus
1609	Cymbeline
1610	The Winter's Tale
1611	The Tempest

III

MOLIÈRE
1622–1673

FRENCH literature of the seventeenth century differs from that of the Elizabethan age in England, as from other periods in France both before and after, by the strict limitation of the audience to which it was addressed. Shakespeare had not only the Queen and the nobility to entertain with his plays, but the common citizens of London and the rude mechanicals, vociferous in the pit, all of them eager for what he could give them, and each class ready to be amused by what he chose, pleasant or unpleasant, to tell them of the others. French classical literature, on the other hand, did not enjoy this freedom. 'It is,' wrote Giraudoux. 'the literature of a single class, and is addressed to the King. All mention of poverty, squalor and physical distress is severely eliminated. Difference of status, the injustice of men's lot, whether given by God or conferred by birth, is passed over in silence. It provides a magnificent description of the glory and pride of the French throne, but says not a word about the real condition of France. On the whole subject of the destitution of the country and the draining away of the nation's strength, it has observed an injunction of silence as rigorously as if it had been imposed by force.'

Molière belonged to the people and knew the French countryside intimately from his travels with his company as a strolling player; he saw the bitter poverty of the peasantry—of those 'strange, wild creatures', as La Bruyère described them, 'male and female, scattered about the fields, burnt black by the sun and bound to the soil which they stir and scratch with tireless persistence: creatures which seem to speak a sort of human language, and reveal, when they stand upright, a human countenance.' Molière was familiar with these creatures, and it is impossible from what we know of his personal life and character, even apart from a few hints in his plays, in *Don Juan* and *Le Misanthrope* especially, not to believe that he felt on his pulses both the cruelty of their lot and, in contrast, the artificiality and emptiness of the life of the Court. Had the circumstances of his time been different, had he enjoyed the freedom of expression which Shakespeare enjoyed, instead of being dependent, like all his contemporaries and compatriots, upon the King's approval, would he have written differently? One cannot answer the question with confidence; nor, perhaps, need one ask it, for what matters is to accept with gratitude what he did, in fact, give us, and to respond to it as it is, while keeping in our minds the circumstances in which it was written and over which he had no control.

Of all writers of comedy in the literature of the world (I exclude Shakespeare, as comedy formed only a part of his work), Molière was the one who had the deepest human sympathy and compassion. Nevertheless he was able to accept the civilization in which he found himself; indeed, he had to accept it—like poor Jane Nightwork, who could not choose but be old. But I mean more than this: I mean that Molière's acceptance was not merely a passive acceptance, but that in spite of the knowledge he possessed of the foundation of misery and destitution upon which that magnificent structure was raised, he was never, in any sense, a 'reformer'. It never occurred to him, as it was to occur to later writers, that a different order of things was possible, or even desirable, however harsh the sufferings of the forgotten peasantry might be and however hopeless their condition. The France of Louis XIV was the most civilized country in Europe from the point of view of the possessors—the only class to have a point of view at all; and Molière was able to write for that class without being crippled by any considerations outside the scope of imaginative literature. His knowledge of the wretchedness of the poor and his compassion for them, kept of necessity from direct expression, can be detected in hints and undertones, and felt as an added enrichment of his work as a whole, but they never made him an alien to the civilization of which he was a part and to which his work was addressed. Molière himself was a *civilized* writer.

Now the word 'civilized' is a distinctive one, and though I could not fully explain what I mean by it without a long discourse, I must give certain indications. To begin with negatives, there are many writers of comparable eminence and some whose work is beyond even Molière's range, to whom the word would not apply. Shakespeare, for instance, is not, in the sense I have in mind, a civilized writer; nor—if I may venture to fly in the face of a large body of critical opinion—is Sophocles. None of the great Romantics are civilized writers, least of all, perhaps, our own. Wordsworth's remark, for instance, that one impulse from a vernal wood could teach him more of Man than could all the philosophers, was in a high degree uncivilized, as are the plays of certain writers today who seem, to put it as mildly as possible, vexed with the world, and represent their characters as floundering about in a sort of swamp of impotent resentment and unfulfilled desires.

The civilized writer has no wish to escape (with Shelley)

> from men and towns
> To the wild wood and the downs,

for the very good reason that he likes towns and enjoys the society of his fellows more than the society of trees. He knows, and is happy to know, that man is a social being, finding his proper satisfaction in intercourse with his kind within the accepted framework of an ordered society. He is not a rebel, but an observer. Though no subject is taboo to him, he maintains the proprieties, keeping his touch light; he never raises his voice, but credits his readers, or his audience, with wits quick enough to take his point, even a hint. For his readers, he assumes, are civilized too, and do not need to be bludgeoned before they take notice. He addresses his peers, thereby paying them a compliment, which it may be hoped that they deserve. He never preaches or declaims; his tone is the tone of talk—of the best talk between equals, where much is assumed but not everything expressed: in such talk the lightest word, or a look or a gesture, may be pregnant with meaning. He deprecates excess of any kind. He is more concerned with this world than the next—because he knows more about it. Being himself both human and humane, he is not shocked at wickedness or folly; but he notes them, perhaps with pity, perhaps with a smile, for he knows that the source of compassion lies very close to the source of laughter—and even of tears. Above all he dislikes any sort of cant or pretentiousness, and looks askance at the lone wolves of the intellect or the spirit, the self-tormentors, the Utopia builders, the dabblers in the intense inane—at all, in short, who do not *belong*, as he belongs.

You will not find a civilized writer in an age of revolution, or at a time when the structure of society is in question. He is the fine flower of an ordered and stable society, of which the basic assumptions are, or at least seem to be, unassailable. And, I need hardly add, the society of which he is the flower must be worthy of him; it must be free from the glooms of persecution and intolerance.

Now it may seem odd to attribute qualities such as these to Molière, who was a merciless critic of the society in which he lived and turned the irresistible weapon of his laughter against so many of its abuses. There is short shrift in Molière's work for the foppery of rank and title divorced from merit—just as the Old Comedy, he says, always had a clownish servant to make the audience laugh, so the modern must have its idiot Marquis to divert the company; and Nicole, one of his admirable domestics who know what's what so much better than their masters, gaily informs M. Jourdain, who is determined to see his daughter at least a marchioness, that the young nobleman in her native village is the awkwardest oaf and the most consummate ass she has ever seen. Poor marquises, they flit, futile and foppish, in and out of play after play, as butts for Molière's half-affectionate ridicule; *toujours des marquis*? as he makes a member of his troupe complain in *L'Impromptu de Versailles*, and retorts, 'Yes, always: what else would you have for a comedy character who is sure to please?' And Sainte-Beuve has reminded us of the posthumous compliment paid to Molière by Napoleon, who, when he revived the titles of nobility after the Revolution, drew the line at marquises. Again, there is little mercy in Molière for the excessive authority of the *père de famille*, or any other distortion of the norm to which society inevitably gives rise; or for the twists and subterfuges of an impotent or frustrated egotism which seeks to compensate itself by pursuit of money or place, by pietism masquerading as piety, or by the assumption of ideals as a cloak to hide the emptiness of the heart. Yet the very fact that Molière's weapon against the abuses of society was laughter is a sufficient indication that he did, as I have said, belong; it is the satirist who in anger, or revulsion, or bitterness, separates himself from society, as Swift did, or the intolerable Juvenal; but Molière was no satirist, he was a writer of comedy, and it is the privilege of the writer of comedy to laugh with love and mockery at what is his own. Moreover it is never society itself that Molière mocks—a book such as *Gulliver's Travels* would have filled him with a sense of outrage, like the ravings of a barbarian; his object is always the anomalies, the real anomalies, of human character, which he presents, sometimes with high seriousness, sometimes with a smile a little wry, often with delight in their sheer absurdity, but never with contempt, as disruptive of the society he tacitly assumes to be the necessary condition of a good life. It is the effect on the stability of the family, which is the basis of society, of the father's avarice, or gullibility, or hypochondria, which gives an added dimension to such plays as *L'Avare, Tartuffe* and *Le Malade Imaginaire.* The comic idea in *Le Misanthrope*, one of the very finest of Molière's plays, lies precisely in the fact that Alceste whose tortured egotism makes him incapable of living in society or of accepting its values, is driven in desperation to abandon it, in order to practise in the wilds—what? The self-abnegation of the hermit? No—but the social virtues! When he announces his intention to seek some desert spot where he will be at liberty to be an 'homme d'honneur', he fails to realize that he will have chosen the very place where the qualities of an 'homme d'honneur', which means much the same as a civilized being, cannot, by definition, have any significance whatever, or even exist. The young woman he loves and urges to accompany him, featherbrained coquette though she is, shows a saner sense of human values when she declares that the thought of solitude lays a cold finger on her heart.

First, then, Molière was a civilized writer. In this he was no more than a child of his age and country. We know—and if we did not know, the events of the past few decades would have taught us—that no civilization is ever really stable, but there have been epochs in history when it has seemed to certain peoples that the society they created was indeed founded upon a rock. The seventeenth century in France (or at least the first three quarters of it) was pre-eminently one of these epochs. The Frenchmen of that century believed in their civilization more than we in England have ever believed in ours. English writers and thinkers have always had a mad streak in them, a dimension of darkness, if I may call it so, a constant sense of the unutterable lying just beyond the borders of speech, an apprehension, expressed or unexpressed, of the fundamental irrationality of things. It runs through all our literature—even Shakespeare, sanest of poets, was haunted by the fear of chaos, and for all his flaming vitality could see men as the stuff of dreams. But French literature, especially the French literature of the seventeenth century, had nothing of this characteristically English quality. No French writer of the Grand Siècle could have exclaimed, with Sir Thomas Browne, 'I love to lose myself in an *O Altitudo*,' or have read Vaughan's statement 'I saw eternity the other night' without wondering if there were not something amiss with the poet's eyes. On the contrary, the effort of French thought was to bring all human experience, including religious experience, within the domain of reason. If one knows what to believe, according to Bossuet, one will know how to act; without clear and distinct ideas, said Descartes, no knowledge is possible. Knowledge increases, but each step into a fresh domain must be confident and firm; at each step an area of darkness must be illuminated and there must be no going forward to lose oneself in that darkness with a thrill of wonder or of fear. If there are dark places in the human soul, they must be explored and explained. Reason, good sense, good taste: those, with the *manners* they imply, were the characteristics of seventeenth century French literature and thought, and with them went, as might be supposed, a respect for authority and 'the rules'. A civilized man must observe the decencies—what is becoming, that is, for a reasonable being. For the conduct of life the authorities were the Church, the power of which increased as the century advanced, and the well-defined structure of society; for literature, there was the general sense amongst men of letters of the Latin past, bringing with it an insistence upon that sort of *deportment* in literature which can be attained only through the most rigorous discipline of thought and language—a perfect clarity and precision. The Académie Française was founded in 1635, and the most uncompromising expression of the literary principles of the age was in the work of Boileau, who saw himself as the modern French Horace—Horace who, in his turn, was the most civilized poet of ancient Rome. In Boileau's *Art Poétique* the term *le bon sens*, the first requirement he tells us of good verse, occurs four times in the first eighty lines. There can be no doubt that he meant us to remember it—in case we had not read Horace, who said exactly the same thing. This insistence upon the dominance of reason and good sense would never have suited the British (whom the French regarded and continue to regard as semi-barbarians), and had we adopted the principles of the French classical age, nine-tenths of our literature would never have been written. Even in France, I suppose, the acceptance of authority had a certain limiting effect; yet there is, in French literature of the Grand Siècle, more pure intelligence and more of the style which is not so much a grace of expression as a quality of thought than in any other literature except that of the great age of Greece.

To this civilization, which also produced such writers as Corneille, La Bruyère, Bossuet, Pascal, La Fontaine and Racine, Molière belonged—wholly and utterly. He accepted it, loved it, laughed at it, described it in all its interwoven social relationships. As much as any writer has ever been, he was a man of his time. French of the French, no other age could have produced him; every sentence he wrote is stamped with the impress of his time and country; and yet—and this is the wonderful thing about him—he can be read by us today without any sense of remoteness; reading him, we find that three hundred years and an alien civilization are no barrier at all. Many great writers of the past, however much we may admire and love them, remain of the past and require of us, before we can make contact with them, a certain intellectual adjustment. But with Molière this, I think, is not so. Molière speaks to us direct, and with a still living voice; child of his age though he was, he seems by a super-abundance of vitality and sheer irrepressible creativeness to overflow its boundaries. How this is so, I shall try to suggest—perhaps it is partly because he never lost sight of what Wordsworth called the 'primary passions' of the human heart, and all his mockery, sometimes tender, sometimes ironic, often boisterous, occasionally with a touch of harshness, was directed against whatever thwarted, or overlaid, or misdirected them.

Molière—his real name was Jean-Baptiste Poquelin—was born in Paris in 1622 of a good bourgeois family. His father was by trade an upholsterer and held an honourable position in the king's household as *valet de chambre-tapissier du Roi*. The appointment was made hereditary and young Poquelin was expected to succeed to it; he did actually do so when his father was too old for the work, but managed to endure it only for a brief time, his interests being elsewhere. While he was still an apprentice in his father's workshop, his grandfather, between whom and the boy there seems to have been a close bond, used to take him to see plays, and it was his grandfather who backed his request to be allowed to continue his education, which up to the age of fourteen or so had been sufficient only to fit him for his trade. For five years he studied under the Jesuits, and also attended the lectures of the celebrated mathematician and materialist philosopher Gassendi. Then he succeeded his father in the household of the king, Louis XIII, but quickly abandoned the post and took himself off to study law in Orleans. Having qualified as an advocate he returned to Paris, where, instead of practising in the profession now open to him, he at once plunged into the real work of his life. The comedies he had watched as a boy with his grandfather at the hôtel de Bourgogne had dwelt in his mind through the years which followed, and he had known even then what it was that he would one day do. Suddenly and decisively he cut himself off from his family, with his father's grudging assent, assumed the name of Molière and put himself at the head of a troupe of players, acting sometimes in Paris and touring extensively in the provinces. It was Molière who wrote most of the plays, produced them all, acted the chief roles and managed the affairs of the company.

These wandering years were the formative period of Molière's career. Yet, having said that, I at once draw back. . . . What impertinence to speak with such apparently confident precision of the growth of creative genius, more mysterious, surely, than the motion of a serpent on a rock or of a ship through the sea. One can map the progress easily enough and trace the influences upon the development, of a man of culture or learning or practical ability; but creative genius eludes such pedantical efforts at precision and psychological cartography. It is at work always, even in idleness, and in all the chances and changes of life. Where did Shakespeare learn most, in Stratford or in London? From the Earl of Southampton or from Anne Hathaway and Judith? At the court or in the Mermaid Tavern? There are minds, even fine ones, which collect their store of knowledge as consciously and deliberately as a geologist looking for specimens, little hammer in hand; there are others which drink it in by the mere process of living, and respond to experience as a garden responds to May sunshine. Molière's mind was of this latter kind. Nevertheless it was during these years of wandering with his troupe that he found much of the stuff of his future work. Challenged once for his innumerable borrowings of plot and incident from other plays ancient or modern, 'I claim my property,' he replied, 'wherever I happen to find it'; that 'property' was lying about in inexhaustible profusion not only in print, but in the faces and voices of the men and women he saw and spoke with, the peasants, stubborn, earthy, ignorant, salty-humoured, their womenfolk wise with the primitive wisdom of instinctive life, the solid bourgeois of the country towns, big men in their small sphere, and bigger still in their own esteem. In this open book Molière read with a quick and passionate sympathy, finding always in his own heart an echo or image of what he read there. He studied people deliberately and consciously, marking their carriage, movement, gesture, and their characteristic mannerisms, to lend immediacy and truth to his own acting, and noting their tricks of speech—as the marvellous vitality and naturalness of the dialogue in his prose plays would tell us; if we did not know it already. But we do know it, for there is a story that during his stay at a certain town in the south of France he used to go every Saturday to the barber's shop, where his own chair awaited him, in order to watch people as they came in; and once he was found sitting for hours in the coach, while it was waiting to start, intently absorbed in the life of the town around him, watching, listening, 'noting the qualities of people'. This habit of watching, silent and abstracted, grew on him with the years; often, even in company, when he had been invited, may be, in the person of the brilliant playwright who might be counted upon to amuse, he would sit without a word. His friend Boileau nicknamed him 'le Contemplateur'; and so he was, brooding incessantly upon the spectacle which the life of men and women unrolled before his eyes; but at the same time, like all men, I suppose, of creative genius—as opposed to those of critical or discursive ability only—like all men, that is, who in plays or novels or poems have been able, through their own sympathy, or understanding, or delight, or compassion, to create images of humanity which glow with an intensity beyond the actual, like Shakespeare himself, say, or Dickens or any other conjuror of the ideal out of the real, he was also living his own fervent life. As I said in my chapter on Shakespeare, a man can, in the last analysis, write only of what he is; Molière was the 'contemplator' not only of the varied pageant of life as others lived it, but also of his own heart. That is the way of great creators and it is out of the secret correspondences between what is without and what is within that their creations arise. The portrait of Molière reproduced in this book is both beautiful and revealing; it is the face of a man familiar with the passions of the heart, a face at once sensuous and refined. He was, it is said, a tallish man, dignified in bearing, grave in manner, with a wide mouth, large nose (that 'rudder of the face', as Coleridge called it), dark complexion, and black, strongly-marked eyebrows, while in temperament he was gentle, kindly and generous. Generous he assuredly was, and not least in the giving of his heart. He was not a man to count the cost of love, and the cost of his love for Armande Béjart, the young girl he married when he was forty, was high indeed. In this, as in much else, he suffered, as all men of fine and sensitive natures must suffer, and his triumph as an artist is that to the end of his life he was able to find matter for gaiety in the knowledge he had won through grief. The laughter in Molière welled up from deep places, and that is why it rings so true. Beethoven —to risk an analogy—was the greatest of tragic composers, yet no man has ever written gayer tunes.

Master of style and language though he was, Molière was never a man of letters in the sense which that phrase evokes. 'Polish your work,' was Boileau's advice to writers, 'and then—polish it again'. Lock up your verses, said Horace, Boileau's master, for nine years, then take them out for a final revision. But that was not Molière's way. He was a player first: his concern was for the success of his troupe, of which he was the leader and manager, and his task was to provide them with matter *pour faire rire* (as he put it) *les honnêtes gens.* All his work was struck off in the heat and with an almost incredible facility: ordered once by the king to present a new piece, he wrote, rehearsed and put it on the stage—the piece was the wholly delightful *L'Amour Médecin*—in five days. *Les Fâcheux*, a comedy in verse, was written and produced within a fortnight. Moreover he bothered hardly more than Shakespeare did about preserving his plays for posterity; he began to print only because somebody else brought out a pirated edition of a particular play, and no collected edition of his work was issued during his life-time. It was a member of his company who did this service for him, nine years after his death, just as Heminge and Condell had done it for Shakespeare. Facility and speed are not necessarily virtues in a writer, and I mention them only because they do, in fact, suggest a distinctive quality of Molière's work. I am not sure if I can explain this, but it does seem to me that just as in life there are certain excellences, both moral and social, which are better achieved without deliberation or conscious thought, so there can be excellences in literature which arise as a by-product of its main intention. Some of the noblest books are built up with the precision of a crystal; every part has its place in the pattern, which, without it, would be incomplete. Others seem to have grown with a sort of instinctive life. One of the charms of Dickens is the irrelevance to his story of half, or more than half, of his characters, which the sheer wealth and inventiveness of his genius could not refrain from creating. His books are like a half-cultivated garden, in which celandines and buttercups ask the beholder if they are not, after all, just as pretty as their more disciplined brethren in the parterres. Now there is little, if any, resemblance between Molière and Dickens, except in the super-abundance of creative energy which each possessed; but it is precisely this super-abundance of creative energy which I want to stress as characteristic of Molière's work. He wrote always for an immediate purpose—*pour faire rire les honnêtes gens* and to provide a living for himself and his company. That was his main intention, always; but what he actually gave us was something incalculably richer than what would have served for an evening's laughter; and it came *by the way*, like a good man's charity; it came out of the inexhaustible fund of his invention.

For thirteen years, from 1645 to 1658, Molière toured the provinces with his company, only occasionally visiting Paris. He staged plays of all sorts, besides his own, tragedy as well as comedy. He wanted, it is said, to become a great tragic actor, but he was unsuccessful in tragic parts and it was not till 1658, when his comedy *L'Etourdi* was revived on the stage of the Petit-Bourbon in Paris, that his personal triumph in the comic role of the valet Mascarille decided his career as an actor; from that time forward he played all the principal roles in his own comedies, with, tradition tells us, an enormous verve and gusto. In the technique of acting he was 'naturalistic' and strongly opposed to any sort of mannerism or rhetorical device in the delivery of his lines, verse or prose. One could guess this by the quality of his own verse, which even in its most finished passages has the easy and supple movement of speech, but he leaves no doubt on the subject by the scene in *L'Impromptu de Versailles* in which he parodies the mannerisms of the rival company of the Hôtel de Bourgogne.

Only four plays survive from his thirteen years of wandering, two of them farcical sketches of the very slightest sort, though even in these the touch of his hand can be felt—and even when they are read, which they were never meant to be. Only a curmudgeon could fail to respond to such generous delight in the absurd. One of the others, the comedy in verse *Le Dépit Amoureux*, has a famous scene on a subject which Molière made peculiarly his own—the lovers' quarrel of which the happy outcome is foreseen from the beginning, and which is parodied, or repeated in a different key, by the lovers' servants, each movement of the scene being light as a feather yet based firmly upon a true and exquisite sense of human feeling. There is a similar scene in *Tartuffe*, and another (the best of all) in *Le Bourgeois Gentilhomme* between Cléonte and Lucile on the one hand and the valet Covielle and his lover Nicole on the other. 'Ah, Lucile,' sighs Cléonte, when the mists of wrath have melted away, 'with one word from your lips you can lull to sleep all the unworthy thoughts of my heart. How easy it is to be persuaded by those we love!' 'Women!' snorts Covielle, 'the damned animals lead us all by the nose!'

It was in the autumn of 1659 that Molière presented to Paris *Les Précieuses Ridicules*. It was the first great turning-point in his career. Molière was incapable of producing work which was merely derivative; whatever he touched he made in some measure his own, simply by his overflowing vitality, his innate sense of the stage, and his ever-watchful and responsive relationship with his audience. Nevertheless he had rested his work hitherto upon theatrical tradition and the familiar themes of the old Italian comedy. Now he threw his props aside. *Les Précieuses* was wholly his own, and its theme was drawn from contemporary life. The play was received with acclamation, and Molière knew that his first real victory was won. 'Henceforth,' he said, 'what are the old models to me? I have only to study life itself.' And he did so: to be sure, he continued to the end to borrow with a happy insouciance plots and incidents which chanced to suit his purpose, but the soul of his plays from that time forward was human character as his own quick and penetrating eye saw it in the life of the world around him. He could filch from some old book every incident for a play, yet make it as new as the dawn of creation, as instant as today, as compulsive as the absurd imaginings of our own hearts. *Les Précieuses Ridicules* is only a short piece, but it belongs to Molière the master. It was billed originally as a farce, but it is much more than that: it is true comedy, being based not upon incident but on character and manners; and who had a better right than Molière, with his fine sense of what is genuine in feeling, his free and frank acceptance of the basic *decencies* ('what befits'—the proper meaning of the word) in human intercourse, to explode with laughter the pretensions of idiot provincial women to a false refinement drawn from the reading of romantic novels? And he does it without a trace of rancour or contempt, in pure gaiety of heart. He is said to have been irresistible in his own playing of Mascarille, the valet who, with his companion, Jodelet, is put up by the rejected lovers to call, in the person of a marquis (*toujours les marquis!*) upon the two young women, to fool them. The dialogue is light as air, rising in a crescendo of absurdity to Mascarille's comments on the verses he wrote that morning ('*Tandis que sans songer à mal*—in all innocence, that is—without malice—like a poor sheep. . . .') and the subsequent conversation with the Vicomte de Jodelet in which he revives the memory of his imagined military exploits ('you remember, Vicomte, how we captured the demilune at the siege of Arras?' 'Demilune? *Demi*lune? Why, Marquis, it was a full moon at least.')

Women, I suppose, no longer model themselves upon

the heroines of romantic fiction; but they have other follies, other sorts of pretentiousness. *Les Précieuses* is as alive as it ever was—and how wholesome a thing is laughter, a better medicine, surely, for human folly than anger, or a sneer.

From the time of *Les Précieuses* ('précieux', by the way, was not a derogatory term until this play had made it so), the scope of Molière's work was rapidly and continuously extended. To the end of his life he wrote plays, and passages of plays, which were pure laughter—*Le Médecin Malgré Lui, M. de Pourceaugnac* and the incomparable *Le Bourgeois Gentilhomme*, to mention but three—but in them there was a growing mastery and ever more evidence of creative power. The young women in *Les Précieuses Ridicules* are not individualized; even the brilliantly imagined Mascarille remains a type; but in these later plays of what I have called pure laughter, plays which give full rein to Molière's exquisite sense of the ludicrous, the characters are no longer types but individuals in the round. Molière has become the poet, in its proper sense of the creator. Plot and incident matter little; he repeats a situation again and again: there are four plays at least in which a father is circumvented in his choice of an unsuitable husband for his daughter, five (if I remember) in which the medical profession is guyed; but these things are framework only, and within it step forth before our eyes a series of unforgettable figures, pulsing with life. Sganarelle the woodcutter—the best of the many Sganarelles—in *Le Médecin Malgré Lui*, quarrelling with his wife ('I, who have four poor little children on my hands . . .' 'Put them down, then') or being approached by Valère who has been led to suppose that he is an eccentric doctor ('Sir, is your name Sganarelle? 'Eh?' 'I asked if you are the gentleman called Sganarelle'. 'Yes and no—it depends on what you want with him'), and entering with enormous gusto into his impersonation of the learned physician ('a shoemaker can't spoil a piece of leather without paying for it, but in *our* profession we can spoil a man for nothing whatever. We never make mistakes: it's the patient's fault if he dies. Moreover there is nothing like the discretion of the dead—not one of them ever complains of the doctor who killed him.'); M. de Pourceaugnac, coming up to Paris from Limoges, full of money and provincial importance, to marry, at her father's wish, a girl he has never seen, and who is already in love with the man of her choice, and the mounting series of fantastic, yet within the atmosphere of the piece wholly credible, devices which are practised by the lovers and their friends with the object of scaring him back to his native town—the doctors who, informed that he is touched in the head, solemnly examine him, the two women who in a fearful assumed jargon one after the other accuse him of having married and abandoned them to bring up alone a troop of children who, a moment later, rush to embrace him with gleeful cries of *Mon Papa, mon Papa!* and, finally, the driving of the poor man to disguise himself as a female to escape the police who have been persuaded that he is a defaulting debtor. It is a wild farce, yet—and this is where the mature Molière never fails us—it is at the same time rooted in reality, for not only is the unfortunate Limousin (Mr. Porker) brought to life with the magical touch of which only the great creative artists know the secret, but the foundation of the play, upon which is built the superstructure of rollicking farce, is as sane as sunrise: it is the prevention of a preposterous marriage in favour of the union of two young people who are equals and happen to love each other. Sganarelle, M. de Pourceaugnac, and then—M. Jourdain. *Le Bourgeois Gentilhomme* is, I suppose, the best known and best loved in this country of all Molière's plays; and no wonder, for it is the richest and most imaginative of the comedies of pure laughter and at the same time the most deeply rooted in reality. The very poetry of the burlesque, it is also, through the secondary characters of the piece, a finely observed picture of middle-class family life, of the society which Molière knew best because he belonged to it. Moreover it is one of the *ballet* comedies, a form which was forced upon Molière by the requirements of the Court and which he accepted with joy and turned to brilliant account. The scenes in which Cleonte pretends to be the son of the Grand Turk asking for the hand of Lucile, and M. Jourdain is initiated into the lofty dignity of a mamamouchi, were suggested to Molière by the visit to Paris the previous year of an envoy from the Sultan, who is said to have caused offence at Court by his arrogance and the excessive luxury of his suite—one Roi Soleil at a time was no doubt felt to be enough. Could the Sultan have seen the play (and understood it) there might, one feels, have been an international incident of some gravity. As for M. Jourdain himself, there is nothing like him in the whole range of European literature. May he continue for ever to have 'the strength of serpents and the wisdom of lions'.

Concurrently with these plays of pure laughter Molière was writing comedies of a different sort, comedies in which the laughter is more inward, an intellectual laughter—when, indeed, it is present at all, and is not replaced by something more akin to a sort of compassionate irony, or, in certain plays such as *Tartuffe* and *Don Juan*, by something a little more astringent. The themes of these plays are serious themes, both in their human and in their social implications; the anomalies of character upon which they are based are not only real, but dangerous; with a change of tone and a shift of emphasis they could be tragic themes. Any human situation can be considered from either of two mutually opposed points of view: call them 'involvement' on the one side, and 'detachment' on the other. The first implies the consideration of the persons concerned primarily as individual souls working out their destiny against odds for which they are not responsible; the second considers them as members of a society whose laws they have, by implication, tacitly accepted and whose troubles, if troubles they have, are seen as denials of that acceptance. In the former, human folly or weakness or vice may appear destructive or terrible; in the latter they appear absurd. It is the special privilege of High Comedy, as distinguished from burlesque on the one hand, and tragedy on the other, to maintain this detachment; starting from a sane, balanced and reasonable belief in the values of the society in which he lives, the writer of comedy, taking his audience into his confidence, observes the deviations from those values—and is amused by them. 'If you believe,' wrote Meredith, 'that our civilization is founded in common sense (and it is the first condition of sanity to believe it), you will, when contemplating men, discern a Spirit overhead. . . . Its common aspect is one of unsolicitous observation, as if surveying a full field and having leisure to dart on its chosen morsels, without any fluttering eagerness. Men's future upon earth does not attract it; their honesty and shapeliness in the present does; and whenever they wax out of proportion, overblown, affected, pretentious, bombastical, hypocritical, pedantic, fantastically delicate; whenever they are at variance with their professions, and violate the unwritten but perceptible laws binding them in consideration one to another; whenever they offend sound reason, fair justice, are false in humility or mined with conceit, individually, or in the bulk—the Spirit overhead will look humanely malign and cast an oblique light on them, followed by laughter. That is the Comic Spirit.' The writer of Comedy also, one may add, maintains the 'unsolicitous observation' of his own passions and of all the movements of his own heart: Molière, at any rate, did so; his own jealousy as well as that of Le Barbouillé and Georges Dandin and Alceste, even his own long-drawn-out sickness, were subjected to the look 'humanely malign', to the oblique light, and to the laughter. That is one measure of his greatness.

The first of these plays was *Tartuffe*. *Tartuffe* is one of Molière's acknowledged masterpieces, but it was not until five years after its first performance before the king in 1664 that permission was granted for its public exhibition. During that time it was considerably altered and enlarged. The reason for the ban is not far to seek, for the play is an attack upon religious hypocrisy, and over-zealous pietists fear nothing so much as ridicule. Much controversy has raged over this brilliant comedy: whom, precisely, was Molière attacking? The Jesuits? the Jansenists? the Compagnie du Saint-Sacrement? Or was he attacking religion itself? The questions are all idle—

except perhaps the last one, which can be answered by a confident No. Molière took his religion lightly and as a matter of course; the bent of his mind was secular, and it was no part of his business as a writer of comedy, or indeed of his temperament, to concern himself with the vague vast ultimates of philosophical or religious beliefs. But he was not a scoffer. He accepted without fuss the religion in which he had been brought up, and to attack it would have been contrary to his nature. The object of his shafts was, as a contemporary put it, not *Dieu, mais les dévots* and the *dévots*—the bigots, and those who concealed the shabbiness of their lives under a cloak of piety—were not unnaturally indignant. Hypocrisy in any of its many guises is a rich theme for the Spirit of Comedy, and Molière joyfully made it his own. 'Hypocrisy,' as he makes Don Juan say in the play of that name, 'is the fashionable vice, and all fashionable vices pass for virtues. Other vices are liable to censure, but hypocrisy is privileged—it shuts all mouths and enjoys a sovereign impunity. How many men do you think I know who protect themselves under the mantle of piety, and in this honoured garb enjoy perfect liberty to be the vilest creatures on earth?' Those are harsh words—and *Don Juan*, unlike most of Molière's work, is a harsh play; but in *Tartuffe* there is no harshness: the theme is serious, but the touch is light, and over it all broods the Comic Spirit, 'humanely malign'. I have not space to quote, but I cannot refrain from reminding those who know the play of the fourth scene in the first act ('*le pauvre homme!*') and of the scene of the handkerchief at the beginning of Act III, when Tartuffe himself first appears after the wonderfully skilful building-up and preparation of the first two acts.

There are two ways of considering a work of art: as a thing-in-itself, and as a reflection of its creator's mind and spirit. The two overlap, and each is fruitful in delight, especially when the work is of a writer with Molière's rich and deep humanity. I have called him a civilized writer, and so indeed he was; but few words could be less adequate to describe him fully. With his quick passions, his many loves, his unrivalled knowledge of the world and of the darker places of the human heart; in spite, too, of the inevitable rough-and-tumble of his life as a player with its petty jealousies and rivalries, and of his own domestic griefs, he retained—I speak of him as he appears in his work—what I can only describe as a fundamental sweetness and soundness, an untarnished clarity of heart and mind. Molière was sane, if ever a man was. By nature unspeculative, and untortured by doubts of the destiny of man in this world or the next, he accepted freely and frankly (like all sensible men) the physical basis of life and the validity of instinct. The twists of mind which attempt to overlay or pervert them are the theme of his mockery in play after play: they make the theme of *L'Ecole des Femmes*, in which Arnolphe tries to ensure the fidelity of his future wife by bringing her up from the age of four in utter ignorance of the world—a play with a brilliantly ingenious plot which, by the simple device of an assumed name and the consequent confusion of identity, allows the girl Agnès and her lover themselves to inform the frustrated Arnolphe of the progress of their loves; a similar theme underlies the profound comedy of *Les Femmes Savantes*, which is much more than a repetition, further elaborated, of *Les Précieuses Ridicules*, and is surely a picture, painted with laughter indeed, though with a somewhat wry laughter, of society women who have their sex in the head because they have not the courage, or have lost the ability, to have it anywhere else. Bélise, in that play, with all the living springs in her dried up, and only the flicker of fantasy left to her half-mad mind, has an almost tragic ludicrousness. The splendid series of domestics—*servantes* or *suivantes*—the Toinettes, Nicoles, Dorines and the rest, are given the same sort of apple-sweet and earthy wisdom, as they speak their minds to their misguided masters. Molière again, like Shakespeare, felt the spiritual and emotional equality of women and men; the tyranny of fathers over daughters and of husbands over wives were alike distasteful to him. The feeling is present in the burlesques and farces, whenever a father's plan to marry his daughter for money or place is circumvented, and it is made articulate in *L'Ecole des Maris* through the clash of sentiment between Sganarelle and his brother Ariste upon the measure of liberty to be given to wives, and the mockery of *les maris loups-garous* (were-wolf husbands) with which the servant Lisette closes the piece. Whatever in human intercourse is free and sweet and kindly and true was dear to Molière, and the sense of these things underlies all his mockery of their opposites.

When he wrote *L'Ecole des Maris*, in 1661, he was about to marry Armande Béjart, a member of his troupe and twenty years his junior. No-one can appreciate Molière's work unless he can understand the quality of his affection for this girl, for the quality of a man's love is conditioned by what he is. Molière's wife was unfaithful to him, and he suffered accordingly. One day a friend found him in great distress, and after a number of attempts prevailed upon him to confess the reason for it. The friend—his name was Chapelle—was a man of the world, and inclined to make light of the matter. 'Come, come,' he said; 'that you of all men should yield to the very weakness you are always laughing at in others! What is more absurd than to love someone who does not respond to your love? In any case, you have an easy means of getting even with your wife for the trouble she has caused you: you have but to shut her up, and you will be able to rest in peace.' 'Have you never been in love?' said Molière. 'Oh yes,' answered his friend; 'I have loved as a sensible man ought; but had my honour required me to be firm, firm I should have been, without fuss. I blush for your irresolution.' 'Then I see,' said Molière, 'that you have never loved at all; you have mistaken the idea of love for love itself.' And he went on to tell his friend that in spite of his anguish of mind he could not help entering with a kind of sympathy even into his wife's infidelities—'When I think,' he said, 'how impossible it is to subdue my love for her, I tell myself that she, perhaps, finds it no less hard not to be a coquette—and then I can but pity rather than blame her. Only those who have really loved can understand this. I refer everything in the world to the image of her which I have in my heart.'

The delicacy of this is surely plain to anyone who knows the difference between reality and sham, and I retell the story to show what I meant when I said that the laughter in Molière welled up from deep places. It is only those who are acquainted with grief whose laughter rings true.

People have speculated upon how much of himself Molière put into his plays. The question, at least in that form, is as idle as the question of whom he was attacking in *Tartuffe*. Of course Molière put himself into his plays—but not directly, for that is never the way of art; but had his own experience been different, he could not have written as he did either of the gaiety or the torment of love: he could not have given us even poor Georges Dandin (*vous l'avez voulu, Georges Dandin . . .*), who comes to the melancholy conclusion that when a man has a bad wife, the best thing he can do is to jump into the river, head first; and he certainly could not have created the marvellously living figure of Alceste in *Le Misanthrope* and the misery of his relationship with the witty and volatile Célimène, that *âme de vingt ans*—like his own Armande. All this is too obvious to dwell upon; but what is less obvious, and more important, is to appreciate the power, which Molière possessed in a supreme degree, of detaching himself, *in the interest of his art*, from the turbulence of his own inner life and of seeing it as a part of the human scene. 'You may estimate your capacity for Comic perception,' wrote Meredith in the essay from which I have already quoted, 'by being able to detect the ridicule of them you love, without loving them less; and by being able to see yourself somewhat ridiculous in dear eyes, and accepting the correction their image of you proposes.'

Le Misanthrope, in many ways the greatest and certainly the most finished of Molière's plays—the play which, though it never moves beyond the mocking yet benign control of the Spirit of Comedy, yet allows, more than any other, certain shadows of a darker import to hover just beyond the confines of the visible scene—was followed within two or three weeks by *Le Médecin Malgré Lui*, that piece of effervescent and delightful absurdity of which I have already spoken. Nothing can better illustrate the nature of Molière's genius than the conjunction of these two plays: it is not only that it shows us its variety; it also indicates the more remarkable fact that the grave and the gay, with all the subtle gradations of each, were not so much alternating or successive moods of Molière's mind, as co-present and interpenetrative. Each was there, all the time, enriching and illuminating the other. That is why one has a sense of spaciousness, of further horizons, even in his slightest pieces. His creative power worked as nature works, where nothing is insignificant because it is in relationship with everything else—and, like nature, it had its surprises, such as the extraordinary scene in *L'Avare*, where Harpagon, the miser, finds that he has been robbed and, seeking the robber in the madness of despair, seizes *his own arm* in the momentary belief that he has caught him. It is a scene beyond burlesque, beyond comedy; in its sudden wildly imaginative quality it touches upon nightmare.

For the latter part of his life Molière was a sick man, though he never ceased to perform the fourfold task of actor, producer, manager and playwright. The nature of his malady is obscure—it is referred to as a *fluxion de poitrine*, which seems to mean some sort of inflammation of the lungs—perhaps chronic bronchitis, possibly tuberculosis. The seat of the malady was almost certainly mental, as Molière apparently knew; for this would account in part for his incessant baiting of the less reputable section of the medical profession, with its assumed omniscience and the absurd remedies commonly advised, for the first conception of *Le Malade Imaginaire* and also, perhaps, for the long speech he puts into the mouth of a quack doctor in *M. de Pour-*

ceaugnac, describing half seriously, half ludicrously, the three forms of melancholia. His own doctor was, however, a close personal friend. It was not the medical profession that Molière attacked, but, as always, the pretentiousness and cant which was to be found there as elsewhere. 'Doctors,' he says; 'they can talk good Latin, and give a Greek name to every disease; but they have not the remotest notion of how to cure a single one of them.' Nature herself, he believed, or tried to believe, was the best medicine. 'Only leave her alone,' as Béralde says in *Le Malade Imaginaire*, 'and she will gradually get herself out of any trouble she may have fallen into. The fatal thing is our own anxiety and impatience—People die of their remedies, never of the disease.'

The undertones and implications of *Le Malade Imaginaire* make it painful reading for those who love Molière. The theme cuts deep into human illusion, but the play nevertheless, with its unfailing sparkle and lightness of dialogue, its ballet interludes part charming, part burlesque, its sustained mockery, and the admirable figure of Toinette, sanest, wittiest and most outspoken of Molière's long gallery of *servantes*, might almost but for the circumstances of its creation, have been for us another of the comedies of pure laughter. But one cannot see it so; underneath the gaiety and the burlesque it has a deeper and more painful resonance; one would have read the play differently had one not known that in the brilliant scene between Argan and his brother Béralde, Molière was, as it were, holding a dialogue with himself, all that was sane and wholesome in him and still in love with life arguing with the spectre which for years, now, had whispered to him of death—

and that the spectre was so soon to have its way. At the first performance on Feb: 10, 1673, Molière, who played the part of Argan, was gravely ill. His wife, with whom he was reconciled, and his friends on the two following nights tried to dissuade him from continuing, but he would not listen to them. With characteristic generosity he refused to deprive his troupe and his stage-workmen of the money which would be lost if he withdrew his play. 'There are fifty poor people,' he said, 'dependent on me for their livelihood, and they shall have it while I can give it them.' On the fourth night he struggled through the performance only with the utmost difficulty. His wife got him back to their lodging. Their friend Baron was with them. 'When my life,' Molière said, 'had both its pleasure and its pain, I thought myself happy; but now that I suffer without a moment's relief, I know it is time to give up the struggle. The pain leaves me no respite—I cannot hold out against it.' A few minutes later he was dead.

It is to the credit of Boileau, whose work was in almost every way the antithesis of Molière's, that he recognized fully and generously the eminence of his friend. One day the king asked him which of the many great writers of the age had, in his opinion, conferred most lustre upon his reign. 'Sire,' said Boileau, 'c'est Molière.' 'I should not have thought it,' was the king's reply; 'but you understand these things better than I do.'

V

SHERIDAN
1751–1816

TO DEFINE greatness satisfactorily is something of a puzzle; for what definition would admit Sheridan into the company of Sophocles, Shakespeare and Molière? It might be better to drop the word altogether and to look for another one: the Greeks, for instance, had a useful word—*amymôn*—which we were taught at school to translate as 'blameless', but which really means good *of its kind*, as one might speak of a good cow, meaning that she had the properties of a cow and not of a horse. Fortunately the pleasures of the mind are as various as the pleasures of the palate, and a taste for burgundy does not preclude a taste for lemonade, provided that the lemonade is blameless and comes from a lemon and not from a bottle. The most stupid—and commonest—fault of criticism is to blame a writer for missing a mark he never aimed at. The proper way to enjoy a book or a play is to submit to it as if, for the moment, it were all: to take what it gives, and not to look around for other gifts which it does not profess to offer. The reputation of Sheridan as a playwright is founded upon two slight comedies and one amusing skit; the two comedies, bright as a bubble and light as air, are as fresh on the modern stage as they were when they were first acted more than a century and a half ago; they have added, and still add, to the 'world's stock of harmless pleasure', and that is a fair title to fame. *The Rivals* and *The School for Scandal* have no reverberations; they do not open to the mind of reader or spectator receding horizons; they touch no depths; they make no revelations; they are the merest butterflies of art. But they are exquisite; within their narrow limits they achieve triumphantly what they set out to achieve. Sheridan, in short, was a blameless playwright, and I could not find it in my heart to exclude him from this book.

The eighteenth century, made illustrious in literary history by the poetry of Pope, the rapid rise of the novel, and, in its closing years, by Boswell's biography of Dr. Johnson, a germinal book of capital importance in English letters, was, in the main, remarkable for extreme poverty in the drama. Of distinguished actors and actresses there were many—the chief of them Garrick, the first player to make a fortune and to be accepted by society—and play-going was becoming increasingly popular; but the plays were poor, and public taste unsure of itself and uncritical.

The brilliant period of drama in the reigns of Elizabeth I and her two successors was abruptly cut short by the coming of the Commonwealth and the edict of 1642 which ordered the suppression of all stage-plays and the closing of the theatres. To the Puritan way of thinking stage-plays—which cannot, indeed, always be wholly serious and uplifting—were an encouragement to vice. Perhaps some plays were—and are; but the Commonwealth government thought it best to be on the safe side, and suppressed the lot. With the Restoration a new drama arose of a very different kind: this was the Artificial Comedy, or Comedy of Manners, as it was called, and reached its culmination in the work of Congreve, whose *Love for Love* and *The Way of the World*—the latter especially—are amongst the world's masterpieces of the Comic Muse. These comedies were written for, and about, a brilliant and idle aristocracy; they were addressed to the head and to the fancy, whereas the richer comedies of Shakespeare were addressed to the understanding—which is head and heart working in unison. Thus they differed from the older comedy in kind, not in degree of excellence. Congreve's wit was unsurpassed, as was his mastery of language. Wit is not a simple term and from the Restoration to the end of the eighteenth century at least it had many shifting connotations. Applied (as it must be) to the plays of Congreve, it might be described as a first cousin of imagination, less richly endowed: imagination penetrates the heart of reality; by seizing correspondences and combining disparate elements it reveals a new truth, or aspect of truth. Wit, no less subtle, no less rapid and adventurous in operation, works by a similar method but with a less penetrative light; it remains content with appearances. Everyone quotes Mirabell's description, in *The Way of the World*, of his lover Millamant, and for the sheer pleasure of copying the words I quote it again: 'Here she comes, i' faith, full sail, with her fan spread and her streamers out, and a shoal of fools for tenders...' How exquisitely the metaphor is sustained and elaborated—not a word but adds a new facet to the diamond. But think, with that description in mind, of Cleopatra in her barge, coming to meet Antony, when she pursed up his heart on the river of Cydnus, and

> the city cast
> Her people out upon her, and Antony,
> Enthron'd i' the market-place, did sit alone
> Whistling to the air, which but for vacancy
> Had gone to gaze on Cleopatra too,
> And made a gap in nature,

and the sort of relationship I have suggested between wit and imagination is not difficult to understand.

This mastery of wit and language Congreve lavished upon the presentation—or creation, rather, for it never existed in so pure an essence in the real world—of a society without heart or conscience or any of the common feelings which make us men. Yet Lamb was right when he declared that he felt the better for reading Congreve. 'I could never,' he wrote, 'connect those sports of a witty fancy in any shape with any result to be drawn from them to imitation in real life. They are a world of themselves almost as much as fairyland.' The characters in the plays 'break through no laws, or conscientious restraints. They know of none. They have got out of Christendom into the land—what shall I call it?—of cuckoldry—the Utopia of gallantry, where pleasure is duty, and the manners perfect freedom. It is altogether a speculative scene of things, which has no reference whatever to the world that is.'

Lamb was writing a hundred years after the first appearance of *The Way of the World*; and changes of taste gave point to his defence. Yet even at the time there was a growing body of opinion which took the brilliant nothings of this kind of comedy in a very different sense. Their most articulate opponent was the parson, Jeremy Collier, who just before the century closed published his *Short View of the Immorality and Profaneness of the*

English stage. Collier seems to have gone one better than Cromwell's Puritans fifty years before. The Puritans, in a grand generalization, condemned the stage as such, and closed the theatres; Collier proceeded to detail and, not content with impugning the morality of plays by such authors as Wycherley and Vanbrough—for which there was some justification—roundly declared that Shakespeare's Ophelia was a character nicely calculated to corrupt an audience. Few studies are more revealing than the vagaries of taste in the matter of the proprieties.

There is no doubt that Collier spoke for many besides himself. By the beginning of the new century the Comedy of Manners was on the way out. Apart from the question of whether that comedy was 'proper' or 'improper' (which in heaven would be a question not of morals but of aesthetics), it was, and was bound by its nature to be, *unpopular*: it was addressed, that is, primarily to the fashionable world. The fashionable world is, at any time, small and exclusive, and as the eighteenth century advanced, more and more people were drawn to the theatre, with the inevitable result that what went on there had to be modified in order to give the new audiences what they wanted.

Garrick, for a quarter of a century the proprietor of Drury Lane, was a great actor, but the public taste for which he catered can be gauged by the fact that in his numerous revivals of Shakespeare he saw fit to alter and rewrite the text. *King Lear*, for instance, was given a happy ending, the old king recovering his wits and Cordelia engaging herself to marry Kent—what happened to the King of France I cannot remember. Even the illustrious Dryden had monkeyed with *The Tempest* and had written his *All for Love* in competition with *Antony and Cleopatra*; indeed the attitude to Shakespeare from the Restoration onwards was an odd one and due in part, I suppose, to the very considerable influence of the French stage upon English playwrights; the French have never cared for Shakespeare—Voltaire, an admirer of England, likened Hamlet's behaviour to the ravings of a drunken savage—and, in spite of Dr. Johnson, we really had to wait for Coleridge and the Germans early in the nineteenth century to recall us to a proper understanding. But in general what the new theatre-going public wanted was a touch of sentiment and bourgeois morality—both admirable things, but not necessarily connected with good dramatic writing. 'Who,' wrote Lamb in the essay from which I have already quoted, 'would forego the true scenic delight, the escape from life, the oblivion of consequences, the holiday barring out the pedant Reflection, those Saturnalia of two or three brief hours, to sit instead at one of our modern plays, to have his coward conscience stimulated with perpetual appeals . . . and his moral vanity pampered with images of notional justice, notional beneficence, lives saved without the spectator's risk, and fortunes given away that cost the author nothing?'

The new Sentimental Comedy, as it was called, filled the theatres, but it was, on the whole, poor stuff. It was the achievement of Goldsmith and Sheridan—first of the humourist and then of the wit—that they admitted a breath of fresh air and a ray of sunlight into the fusty theatre of their time.

Richard Brinsley Sheridan was of Anglo-Irish stock and was born in Dublin in 1751, the third child of a family of four. His grandfather, a clergyman and schoolmaster in Dublin, had been a friend of Swift. The good Doctor was everything an Irishman is supposed to be: much loved and much laughed at, he is said to have been slovenly, indolent and cheerful, knowing books better than men and the value of money least of all—some of which qualities he transmitted to his grandson. Thomas Sheridan, the playwright's father, left to fend for himself while still a very young man, became an actor and a teacher of elocution. The latter seems an odd trade for those days, but Thomas Sheridan, for a time at any rate, was successful at it, and numbered ministers of state amongst his pupils. His friend Dr. Johnson, as might be guesesd, hardly approved of it; Johnson had no very high opinion of actors, anyway, except of Garrick for whom, partly for old acquaintance's sake, he had a half-protective, half-admiring affection, and he was not likely to be much better disposed towards elocution, being perfectly well able to make himself understood without it. 'What influence,' he asked, 'can Mr. Sheridan have upon the language of this great country by his narrow exertions? Sir, it is burning a candle at Dover to show light at Calais.' However, whether Sherry (as his friends called him) had any influence or not upon the language of this great country, he made money by the lessons he gave—and then lost it. Of Mrs. Sheridan little is known, except that she wrote a novel which, Boswell has told us, 'contains an excellent moral, while it inculcates a future state of retribution'; apart from that, what little we hear of her is praise. She died when Richard Brinsley was fifteen.

The young Sheridan was sent with his brother Charles to Harrow, where he in no way distinguished himself, except for high spirits. One of his schoolmasters professed in after years to have detected signs of superior intellect in his idle but charming pupil, and perhaps he did—though schoolmasters are apt, after the event, to claim discernment of this kind, as a salve to their vanity. But Sheridan was destined to idle into fame, and the temper of his schooldays was entirely consonant with his later life. Leaving Harrow when he was seventeen he was reunited with his family who for some years had been in France to escape from creditors. They settled in Bath, then in all its glory as a fashionable resort, where Thomas Sheridan kept himself busy acting and lecturing and gallantly persisting in his efforts to influence the language of his country. His elder son Charles assisted him, but young Sheridan followed his bent and did nothing whatever. He was good-looking and attractive, an amusing talker and a gay companion; everybody liked him, and he liked everybody: at least, he liked to watch everybody, to observe the goings-on of that frivolous and slightly absurd society, 'a chiel among them, taking notes'. But they were kindly notes, for Sheridan was no satirist, and entirely at home amongst the follies he was afterwards to mock so charmingly. Occasionally he wrote, or tried to write, usually in collaboration with a Harrow friend named Halhed, in the vain hope of making a little money, for he was penniless. And he fell in love.

Sheridan's first love makes one of the pleasantest stories in literary history, and has a grace and innocence which would be remarkable in any age and was especially remarkable in his own. Elizabeth Linley when Sheridan met her was sixteen, and already a much admired and successful singer. Her father was the well-known composer and singing-master, and for a number of years past had been the dictator of all musical activities in Bath. Elizabeth was the eldest daughter of this talented family—called by Dr. Burney a nest of nightingales—and her beauty had already attracted a cloud of males, elderly roués and romantic young men, like moths to a candle flame. Sheridan, his friend Halhed and his brother Charles were amongst the moths. Halhed and Charles made no secret of their passion, but Sheridan, who was in fact more deeply involved, was more discreet. At first Elizabeth herself looked upon him as no more than the delightful brother of her bosom friend. But time and circumstances were to change her feelings.

Amongst the innumerable visitors to the Linley household was a certain Captain Matthews, a middle-aged married man, who had manoeuvred Elizabeth into opening a correspondence with him. At first she was flattered and amused by this turn of affairs, but as Matthews became more insistent in his professions of devotion, she grew alarmed, and confided her alarm to Sheridan. Sheridan at once assumed the role of her protector: he made Matthews' acquaintance, obtained from him a pretty clear statement of his purpose, and told Elizabeth of it. Elizabeth was now really frightened; she tried to put a stop to Matthews' attentions, but was met by a threat of suicide. He had also, Sheridan told her, threatened to carry her off by force. It was an intolerable situation for a girl who was still little more than a child. Sheridan, however, was equal to it, and with the connivance of his sister arranged to carry her off himself. It was a fairy-tale elopement, and maintained in all respects the most rigorous notions of honour. Accompanied by an old servant of Sheridan's family, the runaways posted to London, and thence crossed alone to France with the object of finding an asylum for Elizabeth in a convent at St. Quentin. To silence talk they went through a ceremony of marriage at Calais, and immediately afterwards separated. Elizabeth was taken into the convent but was subsequently removed by an English doctor, who put her under his wife's care in Lille. It was some six weeks before the whereabouts of the couple became known in Bath, and Elizabeth's father at once set out to bring her home. Not a word was said either by her or by Sheridan about the marriage, which seems to have been regarded by both of them, at this stage, merely as a means of stopping gossip while they were in France and before Elizabeth had found more conventional protection. Sheridan accompanied Elizabeth and her father back to Bath, where the escapade was received by the large circle of Linley's acquaintance with amused tolerance. Still no word was said of the marriage; apparently both Elizabeth and Sheridan were prepared, or thought they were prepared, to pretend that it had never taken place. Sheridan, indeed, was in love, but being doubtful of the true feelings of Elizabeth he steadfastly refused to take advantage of his situation. Moreover, he had not a penny in the world, and Elizabeth had a father.

Suddenly events took an even more dramatic turn. Shortly after the elopement Matthews had inserted an insulting notice about Sheridan in a Bath news-sheet, and now Sheridan determined to get his blood. Hurrying to London with Charles, he issued his challenge, which was accepted. The antagonists met in an inn parlour, where a confused battle with swords ensued, by candlelight. Matthews got the worst of it and was induced to apologize. Back in Bath news of the duel soon went round and Matthews, ashamed of his defeat, challenged Sheridan to fight again. The second duel developed into a savage scrimmage: Matthews broke his sword on Sheridan's ribs; both men fell, Sheridan with his opponent on top of him, slashing at him with the broken sword. Finally they were separated by their seconds, and Sheridan was carried home, seriously wounded and, as some thought, in danger of his life. Elizabeth at the time was singing in Oxford, and when some weeks later she heard the news which all her friends had tried to conceal, the shock of it wrung from her the cry: 'My husband! My husband!'

Sheridan, nursed back to health by his sisters, was sent by his father to kick his heels in the country, where, it was supposed, he would be more likely to keep out of mischief. Even now there was no general knowledge of his marriage, Elizabeth's anguished exclamation being attributed merely to the excitement of the moment.

Early in 1773, about a year, that is, after the elopement to France, Elizabeth was singing in London, and Sheridan found himself unable any longer to refrain from seeing her. Without his father's knowledge he left the cottage at Waltham and went to extraordinary lengths to procure meetings with Elizabeth, disguising himself as a coachman and driving her back to her lodgings after her performances were over. By one subterfuge or another the meetings continued, and when they could no longer be kept secret Mr. Linley and Sheridan's father were both forced to realize that further opposition was useless. In the April of that year the pair were married—if, indeed, that is the right word; but it does seem that neither of them considered the ceremony at Calais to be a marriage at all, or in any way binding upon them.

When the curtain comes down upon a comedy of this sort, it is assumed that the audience, flattered to tears by the charming sentiment, will not speculate upon the sequel. But in the case of Sheridan and his Elizabeth there is no need to fear what was to come; though he was but twenty-two and she nineteen, and each as warm and impressionable, and as fond of society, as the other, the marriage was a true marriage. Sheridan's temperament was ultimately to ruin him, but for another nineteen years, until Elizabeth died, he had a lover and a companion, with more wisdom than himself to support and guide him.

Meanwhile Sheridan had been writing a little, in a desultory way—a few scenes for projected comedies, and light verse of an evanescent sort such as any cultivated person of that time was supposed to be capable of. For some six months he and his wife lived in a cottage at East Burnham, after which they moved to London and in the winter of the following year took a house in Orchard Street, Portman Square.

Other people's financial affairs are always, I find, a little mysterious, and Sheridan was certainly no exception. His wife, when she married him, had what was left after the French escapade of a small fortune of £3,000. He himself had nothing, and the first thing he did was to forbid Elizabeth to continue her career as a singer. No doubt Elizabeth's father helped to set them up in London; but there was no money coming in, and the house in Orchard Street is said to have been fitted up regardless of expense. A life of lavish entertaining immediately began. There is a story that a friend of Sheridan's remonstrated with him on his extravagance, urging that his means were totally inadequate to such a life of fashionable display. 'My dear friend,' Sheridan replied, 'it *is* my means.'

Fortunately, however, a seed had been lying for a year or two past in Sheridan's mind, and it now suddenly germinated. This seems a fairer way of putting the matter than Sheridan's own, who always liked to pretend that his productions were tossed off with the utmost casualness and ease, hardly interrupting his life of fashionable indolence and pleasure. 'There will be a comedy of mine', he wrote to Linley, 'in rehearsal at Covent Garden within a few days . . . I had not written a line of it two months ago, except a scene or two which I believe you have seen in an odd act of a little farce.' The comedy was *The Rivals*, and it was performed at Covent Garden in the January of 1775. On the first night the piece failed; but the manager of the theatre had confidence in its qualities, and after very considerable and judicious cutting, and the substitution of a different actor from the one who had played the part of Sir Lucius, it was brought back upon the stage, and succeeded. A month later it was produced in Bath where it was received enthusiastically. Since then its popularity has never declined.

The Rivals was a return to the old Comedy of Manners, modified by a certain concession to the changed taste of the time for the 'sentimental'. Happily the sentiment—introduced mainly through the character of Faulkland—is handled with sufficient lightness and gaiety not to spoil the whole. But any formal criticism of the play seems pendantical, and beside the point. The thing is a bubble—a nothing; yet it has its place in the dramatic literature of the world. Without roots in reality, it lives, and will continue to live; of irrepressible gaiety, it is made of laughter which is wholly devoid of irony and leaves no sting. One is the better for such laughter.

The plot is ingenious enough. The two rivals (as most of my readers will know) are but one man, Captain Absolute pretending to be the penniless ensign Beverley in order to win the affection of the romantic Lydia, who cannot endure the prospect of a safe and conventional love affair, while his rich father, Sir Anthony, wishes to marry him to her in his own, and unacceptable, person. But who cares about the plot? The delightfulness of the play is wholly in the dialogue, with its unfailing effervescence, its feather-light touch and heady sparkle like the bubbles in wine. 'Yes, Jack' (says Sir Anthony to his son), 'the independence I was talking of is by a marriage—the fortune is saddled with a wife—but I suppose that makes no difference.

Jack: Sir! Sir! You amaze me!

Sir Anth: Why, what the devil's the matter with the fool? Just now you were all gratitude and duty.

Jack: I was, Sir—you talked to me of independence and a fortune, but not a word of a wife.

Sir Anth: Why—what difference does that make? Odds life, Sir, if you have the estate, you must take it with the live stock on it, as it stands.

Jack: If my happiness is to be the price, I must beg leave to decline the purchase. Pray, Sir, who is the lady?

Sir Anth: What's that to you, Sir? Come, give me your promise to love, and to marry her directly.

Jack: Sure, Sir, this is not very reasonable, to summon my affections for a lady I know nothing of.

Sir Anth: I am sure, Sir, 'tis more unreasonable in you to *object* to a lady you know nothing of....'

Sir Anthony, despite such bursts of unanswerable, Alice-in-Wonderland logic, is, one must admit, a stage father of very familiar pattern, as is Captain Jack Absolute, his son. Indeed, all the characters of the play are conventional characters; but they have passed through the crucible of Sheridan's wit, and come out new. Even Mrs. Malaprop (whose name has given a new word to our language) had her fore-runners—yet she stands unchallenged in her kind through the sheer fertility of Sheridan's delighted invention. He cannot let her alone; he plays with her like a child with a toy, tosses her up and catches her, twists her about and tries again—hit or miss, but nearly always hit—to our unflagging entertainment: whether she assures Sir Lucius that her love shall never be miscellaneous and that female punctuation forbids her to say more, exclaims that the Captain is the very pineapple of politeness, reprehends the use of her oracular tongue and a nice derangement of epitaphs, sighs that Lydia is as headstrong as an allegory on the banks of the Nile, or shudders, when the duel is in prospect, at the thought of the fine suicide, paracide and salivation going on in the fields. Moreover, by a delicate touch of dramatic art, dear Mrs. Malaprop is allowed in the end to show herself to be by no means wholly a fool.

Yet, in all this nonsense, there is a picture of a society, now for ever gone. I said the play has no roots in reality: neither has it; but a better image might be to call it cut flowers—for a brief moment as bright as when they grew. The thing has style: it is as *civilized* as Molière, though without a trace of Molière's wisdom or knowledge of the human heart.

In the same year Sheridan produced two other plays

—both now forgotten: the farce *St. Patrick's Day* and the light opera, *The Duenna*. Personally, I cannot quite forget *St. Patrick's Day*, if only for Mrs. Bridget's reason for deprecating soldier husbands: 'O barbarous! to want a husband that may wed you today, and be sent the Lord knows where before night; then in a twelve-month perhaps to have him come *like a Colossus*, with one leg at New York and the other at Chelsea Hospital . . . No, give me a husband that knows where his limbs are, though he wants the use of them.' *The Duenna*, strangely enough, was immensely successful, and considered superior to *The Beggar's Opera* which had first appeared nearly fifty years before, and which Byron in his letters refers to as 'that St. Giles' lampoon.' The music (of which I know nothing) for *The Duenna* was written by Sheridan's father-in-law, Linley. Perhaps it was that which made it popular, for the lyrics are nothing much. Public taste has surely been right in preserving *The Beggar's Opera* for posterity.

It was at this time, the end of the year 1775, that Garrick announced his intention of selling his share in the patent of Drury Lane Theatre. Sheridan, now twenty-four years old, had made money by his successes and seemed to have a brilliant future before him, so with characteristic rashness he determined to acquire a controlling interest in the theatre himself. He managed in some unspecified way to raise £10,000—what he had earned by his plays, though considerable, could hardly have paid for more than his current expenses—and with the assistance of Linley and of a certain Dr. Ford, who each put up a similar sum, he bought Garrick out and took upon himself, with the consent of his partners, full responsibility for the control of the great enterprise.

Garrick had made a fortune out of Drury Lane, and as Covent Garden was the only other licensed theatre in London at that time, any other competent person ought to have been able to do the same. Sheridan, however, lacked all the qualities of a man of business; brilliant, sanguine and feckless, the best talker in London and the gayest companion, a man of genius able to work only when some unpredictable spark set his mind on fire, he was incapable of the drudgery and close attention to detail which a business enterprise requires. Garrick wanted Sheridan to succeed him; but Garrick did not know his man. Sheridan's control of the great theatre consisted for the most part in doing nothing whatever and hoping for the best.

Nevertheless, before serious decay set in, there was to be one triumph, and that a great one. In the early summer of 1777, rather more than a year after Sheridan had assumed control, *The School for Scandal* was produced.

The actual writing of *The School for Scandal* was even more hurried than that of *The Rivals*, the last act being put into the hands of the players only five days before the opening night. But in another sense the play had been the work of years. Sheridan had pecked at it, and brooded over it, ever since he first discovered his talent for comedy; he had written scenes, and sketches for scenes, some of which were retained, others discarded. Two separate plots seem to have been running concurrently in his head, one in which the scandalmongers controlled the action and another concerning an old man and his young wife and two brothers, one virtuous, the other a hypocrite, who entangle themselves in her destiny. Had all been well at Drury Lane, nobody knows how much longer Sheridan would have played with his ideas; but all was not well: actors and the other shareholders alike were impatient for something which would steal the glory of *The Rivals* from Covent Garden and restore the already diminished lustre of Drury Lane. Sheridan knew that the effort must be made, and, in characteristic fashion, made it. The two plots were amalgamated, and the work which had occupied his thoughts for so long was rapidly completed. The play, which is Sheridan's masterpiece, was received with acclamation.

The greatest comedies of the world are based upon a perception of the real anomalies of human character. Alceste, for instance, in Molière's *Misanthrope,* is a good man: how is it, then, that he can also be absurd? Falstaff is a rogue and a libertine, soaked in sack; yet we laugh ourselves into loving him. One cannot, it seems, judge a man by an arithmetical assessment of his virtues and vices: the sum, for some delightful reason, always comes out wrong. Of this quality of perception there is in *The School for Scandal* not a trace, any more than there is in its predecessor, *The Rivals.* The chief characters are all stock characters of comedy—the elderly husband, the giddy young wife, the spendthrift young man with a heart of gold; but though the play does not illuminate the heart, as the greatest comedies do, with laughter, it does present a picture of a certain aspect of society with unsurpassed brilliance and precision. The world it presents is, of course, the world of idle fashion—like that of Congreve; but whereas Congreve painted society as if it were a thing-in-itself, self-sufficient, and with no threads, visible or invisible, to connect it with another life beyond, Sheridan, catching the altered tone of his day, stands a little apart from his creation, casts upon it an eye of half-whimsical criticism, and allows us to believe, even while the play is playing, and we are enjoying the polished wit of the scandalous tongues, that fashionable society, with its inevitable boredoms and frivolities, is, however gay and brilliant the picture it presents, both corrupt and corrupting. Sheridan himself might well have denied this: but it is true—it was the debt which he had perforce to pay to the Sentimental Comedy which had held the stage for so long.

The School for Scandal makes one laugh less than *The Rivals*—and less, perhaps, than certain pieces of inspired nonsense which occur in Sheridan's minor plays, like for instance poor Dr. Rosy's lament, in *St. Patrick's Day*, over his wife who was carried off by an inhuman dropsy: 'gone never to return, and left no pledge of our loves behind—no little babe to hang like a label round papa's neck'; but the *inward* laughter is subtler and more all-pervading, and for plot and stage-effect it is greatly superior. Sheridan had the true playwright's eye for a situation, and in the whole range of comedy there are few better contrived or more amusing scenes than the 'screen' scene of this play, in which all the chief characters are brought together at the crisis of their fortunes, and the knots are untied. But, when all is said, it is the unfailing point, wit and polish of the dialogue which make *The School for Scandal* a classic of the English stage; the talk is as bright as a button and as sharp as a rapier; it keeps the audience on edge with expectation, which it continually satisfies. 'What makes you impatient of Sir Peter's temper,' says Joseph to Lady Teazle, 'and outrageous at his suspicions'? Why, the very consciousness of your innocence.'

Lady T.: 'Tis very true.

Joseph: Now, my dear Lady Teazle, if you would but once make a trifling *faux pas*, you can't conceive how cautious you would grow, and how ready to humour and agree with your husband.

Lady T.: Do you think so?

Joseph: Oh I am sure on 't; and then you would find all scandal would cease at once; for, in short, your character at present is like a person in a plethora, absolutely dying from too much health.

Lady T.: So, so; then I perceive your prescription is, that I must sin in my own defence, and part with my virtue to preserve my reputation?

Joseph: Exactly so, upon my credit, ma'am.'

Taste changes, the forms of society—and hence the themes upon which comedy is built—shift and dislimn like the architecture of clouds, but this play keeps its point and freshness. The infallible preservative is style.

The success of *The School for Scandal* put Drury Lane temporarily on its feet again. Sheridan, who had sunk all he possessed and all he could borrow in the venture, now looked forward to a golden future. He lived the life of a wealthy man, and entertained an increasing number of friends and acquaintances on a more and more lavish scale, visiting, in his turn, the houses of the great, where his talk and his charm always found him a welcome. His ambition grew. A successful playwright, or man of letters of any other kind, enjoyed less consideration from society in the eighteenth century than perhaps he does today, and Sheridan was determined, if he could, to win fame and fortune and position in a wider field. His thoughts accordingly began to turn towards politics. But meanwhile his brief but brilliant literary career was to have one more triumph, though a minor one. In the same year as *The School for Scandal* Sheridan's last play of any importance, *The Critic*, was produced.

It may well be that the stories, which all Sheridan's biographers tell, of the haphazard manner in which his plays were flung together at the last minute were encouraged by Sheridan himself, who liked to adopt the pose of 'writing like a gentleman', much as Byron liked his friends to believe that he composed his *Giaour* and *Lara*, and so on, while he was shaving in the morning after a night of revelry at some ball or rout. There is in most of us a touch of snobbery which finds a certain seductiveness in the idea of such dandified brilliance. Sheridan had no desire to appear as the professional man of letters; much more to his taste was the reputation of a society wit whose by-work chanced to be the best comedy of his century. Nor was the pose, if pose it was, without foundation in reality, and it helps to account both for virtues and for the limitations of his work. The method of composition of *The Critic* seems by all accounts to have been 'gentlemanly' to excess: three days before the play was due to appear, the last scene was still unwritten. Sheridan's co-proprietors, Linley and Ford, were on tenterhooks with anxiety; the actors were in despair. For weeks past King, who was stage-manager and was to play Puff, had been pestering the reluctant author to do his duty, but in vain. 'At last,' we are told, 'Mr. Linley hit upon a strategem. A night rehearsal was ordered, and Sheridan having dined with Linley was prevailed upon to go. When they were on the stage, King whispered to Sheridan that he had something to communicate, and begged that he would step into the second greenroom. Accordingly Sheridan went, and found there a table with pens, ink and paper, a good fire, an armchair at the table and two bottles of claret, with a dish of anchovy sandwiches. The moment he got into the room, King stepped out and locked the door, immediately after which Linley and Ford came up and told the author that until he had written the scene he would be kept where he was. Sheridan took this decided measure in good part; he ate the anchovies, finished the claret, wrote the scene, and laughed heartily at the ingenuity of the contrivance.'

The Critic or *A Tragedy Rehearsed* is a skit on the most abject aspect of the contemporary theatre. For us, some of its point is inevitably blunted, as our own theatre, even when it is abject, is abject in a different way. We no longer write tragedies in mock-Elizabethan fustian. Nevertheless Sheridan cannot fail to be entertaining. The skit is as high-spirited as *The Rivals*, and reads like a glorified charade. The first act, with the admirably devised portrait of Sir Fretful Plagiary and the explications of Mr. Puff of the fine art of puffing a forthcoming play, is as sparkling and as tart in flavour as anything Sheridan wrote, and the second act, in which Mr. Puff's new tragedy is rehearsed, with a running commentary from the author himself and two unsympathetic critics, is a splendid joke.

> *Puff*: Now enter Tilburina!
> *Sneer*: Egad, the business comes in quick here.
> *Puff*: Yes, Sir—now she comes in stark mad in white satin.
> *Sneer*: Why in white satin?
> *Puff*: O Lord, Sir, when a heroine goes mad, she always goes into white satin—don't she, Dangle?
> *Dangle*: Always—its a rule . . .

(*Enter* Tilburina *and* Confidant, *mad, according to custom*)

Sneer: But what the deuce—is the confidant to be mad too?

Puff: To be sure she is—the confidant is always to do whatever her mistress does . . .

Tilburina: . . . Is this a grasshopper? Ah, no, it is my Whiskerandos—you shall not keep him—An oyster may be crossed in love—who say's

A whale's a bird? Ha! did you call, my love?
He's here! He's there! He's everywhere!
Ah me! He's nowhere!

(*Exit* Tilburina)

I think one is aware, reading that passage, of the anchovy sandwiches and the two bottles of claret.

Apart from the plays I have mentioned, Sheridan, before he wrote *The School for Scandal*, had adapted a comedy of Vanburgh's, which he called *A Trip to Scarborough*, and he produced, after *The Critic*, a dreary bread-and-butter tragedy called *Pizarro*, which is deservedly forgotten, being much the kind of stuff which was so effectively burlesqued in *The Critic*. *The Critic* was his last farewell to the stage which for a few short years he had so brilliantly adorned. He still had thirty-seven years to live, but to literature he contributed nothing more.

The rest of his life-story must be briefly told. In 1780 he was elected to Parliament in the Whig interest, and became a close friend of Charles James Fox and afterwards of Burke. He was an under-secretary of State in the Rockingham ministry, and later Secretary of the Treasury under the Coalition. In politics he was always on the liberal and reforming side, and, to his credit, he made no money out of office. With his wit, command of language and sense of style he was naturally a speaker of the first quality. One speech of his, that which he made in the House in support of the trial of Warren Hastings, has gone down into history. Fox said of it: 'All that I have ever heard—all that I have ever read—when compared with it dwindle into nothing and vanish like vapour before the sun.' The core of the speech—it lasted for five and a half hours—was a protest against the cruel treatment of the Princesses of Oude, whom Hastings had imprisoned. So great was the effect of it, even on those who were most strongly prepossessed in Hastings' favour, that the debate was adjourned to give time for emotion to cool before a vote was taken. With such powers, and with a foot already on the ladder to high place, it seemed as if no eminence were impossible for Sheridan to attain. But Sheridan was not made for the mountain tops, either in literature or in politics; in literature, though his best was supreme in its kind, he had, quite simply, not enough to say to be amongst the greatest, and in politics, though he had the desire for true eminence, he lacked the vision to attain it. Moreover he was never capable of the application and drudgery which are the necessary basis of any work of supreme quality of whatsoever kind. He was a butterfly of both literature and politics. Wholly characteristic of him was his management of Drury Lane: the thing should have been a gold mine, as it was to Garrick, and as Sheridan hoped it would prove to himself. But hoping was not enough, and as time went on he could not bother even to open his busines letters—let alone answer them.

In 1792 his wife Elizabeth died; three years later he married again, but the second marriage brought him

MOLIERE

From a drawing by Ronjat, after the painting attributed to Pierre Mignard

Mander & Mitchenson Theatre Collection

SHERIDAN

From an engraving by R. Hicks after the portrait by Sir Joshua Reynolds

little happiness. One evening in the spring of 1809 during a debate in the House of Commons news was brought that the rebuilt theatre in Drury Lane was on fire. Sheridan hurried to the spot, knowing that for him this was the end. A few hours later he was found in one of the Covent Garden coffee-houses, trying to drink himself insensible; an actor from the theatre, who had been watching the conflagration, cried out at the sight of him, and attempted to remonstrate. But 'what?' was Sheridan's answer; 'surely a man may be allowed to take a glass of wine by his own fireside.' Recovery from this final and crushing financial loss was impossible.

Nevertheless he continued to live the social life which had become a necessity to him, bringing to it a gaiety which was often a cloak to despair. Byron, who knew him well, describes in a letter to Thomas Moore a dinner-party at which they were both present, and which must have resembled many another. The party, he wrote, 'was first silent, then talky, then argumentative, then disputatious, then unintelligible, then altogethery, then inarticulate, and then drunk. When we had reached the last step of this glorious ladder, it was difficult to get down again without stumbling; and, to crown all, Kinnaird and I had to conduct Sheridan down a damned corkscrew staircase . . . to which no legs, however crooked, could possibly accommodate themselves. We deposited him safe at home, where his man, evidently used to the business, waited to receive him in the hall . . . Perhaps you heard of a late answer of Sheridan to the watchman who found him bereft of that divine particle of air called reason. He, the watchman, who found Sherry in the street, fuddled and bewildered, and almost insensible, "Who are *you* sir?"—no answer. "What's your name?"—Answer, in a slow, deliberate and impassive tone: "Wilberforce!" Is not that Sherry all over? Poor fellow, his very dregs are better than the "first sprightly runnings" of others.'

But for Sheridan it was a hopeless struggle against the gathering darkness and the bitter knowledge that his day was over. Byron, some two years before Sheridan's death, tells another story of him, this time a moving one: 'The other night,' he wrote 'we were all delivering our respective and various opinions on him, and mine was this: "Whatever Sheridan has done or chosen to do has been, *par excellence*, always the best of its kind. He has written the best comedy (*The School for Scandal*), the best drama (in my mind far before that St. Giles' lampoon, the *Beggar's Opera*), the best farce (*The Critic*—it is only too good for a farce), and the best Address (Monologue on Garrick), and, to crown all, delivered the very best Oration (the famous Begum speech) ever conceived or heard in this country." Somebody told Sheridan this the next day, and on hearing it he burst into tears. Poor Brinsley! if they were tears of pleasure, I would rather have said these few, but most sincere, words than have written the Iliad.'

Always in debt even in his days of prosperity, Sheridan now sank deeper and deeper into the mire with no prospect of extrication; soon after the destruction of the theatre, he had lost his seat in Parliament, which had at least protected him from arrest, so there was no longer any escape from his creditors; bailiffs took possession of his house, and it was gradually stripped of everything it contained. The noble friends of whom he had many, including the Prince Regent, began to fall away and did nothing to help him—indeed, there was nothing to be done, except to await death as a release. It came, after a short illness, on July 7, 1816. Thus the bankrupt actor's son, the penniless youth, the adventurous and romantic lover, the brilliant playwright, the wit and darling of society, the statesman who at least promised great things, died at last in misery. His spirit may well have looked down, not without irony, on the funeral procession of royalty, peers of the realm and all the noblest in the land, which followed the coffin containing his body to its resting-place in Westminster Abbey.

V

IBSEN

It so happens that I write this chapter on Ibsen immediately after finishing my chapter on Molière, and I am reminded of Professor G. F. Bradley who, writing of Jane Austen, declared that though he did not know whether *Pride and Prejudice* or *Mansfield Park* was the better novel, he knew very well indeed which he liked best. Placing books and authors in an order of merit is always, I suppose, a somewhat futile task, and I have no idea whether Molière was a greater playwright than Ibsen, or Ibsen than Molière; but I have no doubt about which of the two I prefer.

The huge figure of Ibsen dominates the dramatic literature of nineteenth century Europe. His achievement was great, his influence upon the course the drama was to pursue greater still. No student of the theatre, whether he likes his plays or loathes them, can afford to ignore him. Having first made his name in his native Norway as a poet, he proceeded by a series of prose plays to shatter the complacency of theatre audiences in every country of Europe and to reveal to them potentialities which they had never suspected the drama to possess. In the six or seven great plays he wrote in his middle and later life he achieved this pre-eminence by a superb sense of theatrical effect, an unequalled mastery of dramatic construction, a powerful, though limited, imagination, and a choice of themes which profoundly disturbed the proprieties and conventions of his age. Ibsen was a giant; some think he was an ogre; but, whether he was giant or ogre, he has to be reckoned with. The greatest tragic literature, as I suggested in my chapters on Sophocles and Shakespeare, is, in its effect, liberating; it exalts and purifies. Aristotle, a critic with a very cool head in a nation aflame with every passion under the sun, declared that the tragic drama, through pity and terror, purges the heart. Ibsen's plays, both tragedies and tragi-comedies, have a different effect: they come down on the spirit like a ton of bricks. A man writes out of what he knows and of what he is; the plays which have made Ibsen famous, such plays as *Ghosts*, *The Wild Duck*, *John Gabriel Borkman*, *Little Eyolf*, were the plays of a man haunted by guilt and devoured by resentment who abandoned first his family, then his country, then his religion, then nearly all his friends and, finally, his wife, from whom in old age he was estranged, in order to concentrate on the one thing which was important to him—his art. 'All or nothing' was a phrase often on Ibsen's lips; it is a dangerous phrase in spite of its heroic sound—for it may suddenly turn into All *and* Nothing, a terrible emptiness. The creative artist who proceeds by separation, exclusion and sacrifice may find that he is walking only towards a spiritual vacancy. In the plays of Ibsen's maturity there is indeed a terrible emptiness, a cold negation. 'All men,' said Ibsen, at the time of writing his *Ghosts*, 'have failed'; and he certainly included himself in that lamentable statement. The effect of these plays, hewn out of rock like the coast of his own Norway and no less barren and dark—plays without hope or belief or happy illusion, in which ordinary men and women—no great sinners—move under a blind necessity to inevitable destruction, is like a touch of ice on the heart, or the worse horror of the Great Boyg which Peer Gynt encountered on the mountain, the Great Boyg himself, most frightful of the trolls, vast, shapeless, faceless, waiting to envelope the lonely traveller in its invisible and killing embrace.

But before Ibsen could write these tremendous but deathly plays, he had, like lesser men, to learn his trade, and he learnt it in a hard school.

He was born in 1828 in the Norwegian coast town of Skien, seventy miles south-west of Oslo. His father, a man of narrow and conventional piety, had made money in commerce, and was a respected figure in the town. Norway is a largish country—its coastline is double the length of England and Scotland combined—and its population in those days was a bare million of people, scattered about in small communities isolated from each other by mountain and fiord and with little communication with the outside world. The people were farmers, fishermen, sailors and shipbuilders, and the few prosperous bourgeois families dominated the local politics of their respective settlements, which tended to seem matters of greater concern than national affairs, as the country was still under the Swedish crown and had no say in foreign policy. Physically Norway is a land of terror and beauty, with its inaccessible mountains, lonely forests and the untranquil sea running deep inland in innumerable fiords. It had always been haunted by folk-lore and legend, and ghosts and trolls moved in the imagination of its unlettered people with all the force of living presences.

When Ibsen was eight years old his father went bankrupt and the family had to leave home and settle on a small farm outside Skien, which was all that remained of the family property. The blow was a shattering one, not least to young Ibsen himself, who was by no means of the sort to lessen a grief by sharing it; the effect on him, even at that early age, seems to have been chiefly an abiding sense of humiliation and resentment. At the age of sixteen he left home for Grimstad, some fifty miles away along the coast, where he earned a meagre living as an apprentice in a chemist's shop. He never wrote to his family—except once or twice to his sister Hedvig—during the rest of his life, and revisited them on a single occasion only. In Grimstad the brilliant but unhappy lad led an obscure and frustrated existence, working off his spleen by writing verse lampoons on the local bigwigs. After two years he found himself the father of an illegitimate son by a servant girl. The law compelled him to contribute to the child's maintenance, for fourteen years; but he took no personal interest in it whatsoever. The sense of guilt engendered by this incident and fostered by his puritan upbringing and a lack of generosity in his own nature seems to have remained with him through life. The abiding potency of old sins which refuse to die and the fear of retribution were to become a basic theme in his work. At the present day we take such things more casually—perhaps for the better, perhaps for the worse; but society in Grimstad in the 1840's was even more rigid and censorious than it was in Skien, and the bankrupt's son who had had a clandestine liaison with a servant-girl ten years his senior was not likely to find in it a favourable reception. Already an outcast, he was not slow to move into opposition. Conscious of his intellectual power, he became the censor of his censors, well aware of the hypocrisies, little or big, upon which society is everywhere, and necessarily, founded. Acutely sensitive and of a nature unwarmed by the generous affections, he was already, at this early age, turned in upon himself. That self was indeed a continent, though a bleak one, and he was never to escape from it. It was that imprisonment which brought its terrible retribution, and drew from him in the end the denial of life, that *Nay* at once passionate and cold, which lies at the heart of his latest plays.

Everyone knows the story of Carlyle's young friend who was reported to have declared that she accepted the Universe, and the old philosopher's grimly chuckled comment: 'Gad, she'd better.' Ibsen was less complacent; he was a rebel from the first, against his family, against society, against the very balance of pleasure and pain in human destiny, and finally against himself. Nevertheless in these early years there was a certain intellectual idealism in his rebellion; he took fire at the revolution of 1848 in France, when he was twenty, and wrote his first verse play under the inspiration of that event. The play was *Catiline*, a sympathetic study of that appalling thug who with a sharked-up army of lawless resolutes tried to overthrow the government in Rome. A friend of Ibsen's paid for its publication; but nobody bought it, and the copies were sold to a grocer for wrapping-paper. Intellectual idealism is a common thing in the young, and a good one when the motives are right; Ibsen's idealism may have started in resentment, but he did have genuine dreams of a better world and a freer society, and the romantic patriotism which made him long for an independent and united Norway, worthy of her legendary past, was, while it lasted, true enough.

In these days Ibsen was often hungry; nevertheless, soon after he had written his *Catiline* he found means to go to Oslo where he worked, unsuccessfully, for matriculation, and made some friends who were useful to him, amongst them the writer Björnsen. Björnsen was younger than Ibsen and at once recognized the power that was in him; his encouragement was invaluable, and though the friendship had its ups and downs, as when the younger man thought, perhaps rightly, that Ibsen was guying him in some of his later work, it was lifelong. Meanwhile Ibsen continued to write—political skits, verses, and another play which was given a performance in the Oslo theatre. But there was no money, and he might actually have starved had he not, through the influence of friends, been offered the post of Director of the national theatre in Bergen at a salary of 30s. a week. His work in the theatre was to train the actors, produce the plays and contribute plays of his own; in idea this might have been just what Ibsen needed: nationalism was already stirring, and the Bergen theatre owed its existence to the vision of a musician named Ole Bull, who hoped that it might contribute something towards the freeing of Norwegian culture from the domination of the Danes. Such a purpose had, at the time, Ibsen's enthusiastic support. It proved, however, only another heartbreak: Ibsen was too timid to tell his players of their faults and his own plays, founded on the old heroic legends of Norway, were failures. 'He was always kindly and polite,' wrote the actress Lucia Wolf, 'but in his kindness there was something which invariably made me, at any rate, finish my talk with him as quickly as I possibly could. . . . Wrapped in his long cloak he would pace all the time up and down and, if addressed by anyone, would retreat into that cloak like a snail into its shell.' None the less, the experience at Bergen was valuable to him, and when, after six years had passed, a national theatre was opened in Oslo as a rival to the existing Danish theatre there, Ibsen was offered the directorship of it, and accepted. The new field was no more fruitful than the old, though two of his plays on national-romantic themes, *The Vikings at Helgeland* and *The Pretenders*, won a certain recognition. But the first play of a more individual kind, in which Ibsen gave direct expression to some of his ideas about contemporary society, caused an uproar and raised the country against him. This play was *Love's Comedy*, and the burden of it was an attack upon the clergy and, more particularly, upon the institution of marriage. It was written almost immediately after his own marriage to Susanna Thoresen, and was followed by the financial collapse and closing of the Oslo theatre. Ibsen was not the first youthful idealist and, no doubt, will not be the last, to proclaim the incompatibility of love and marriage—'the longest journey'. To do so is an endemic malady of the poetic young, and Ibsen fell for it. One cannot blame him: the play was written with verve and even a touch of humour, and the views it contained must be judged from a sense of values and a definition of terms which only experience can provide grounds for. 'I have represented in it,' Ibsen wrote in a letter, 'the contrast in our present state of society between the actual and the ideal in all that relates to love and marriage.' The words have a familiar ring: how many of the young and ardent have had to learn the falsity of that distinction in all matters connected with the human heart, indeed the peril of making such a distinction at all? Most ideals are a menace to life unless they are seen through the veil of the actual. Ibsen certainly hoped to flutter the dovecotes by the unconventionality of this piece, but he was hardly prepared for the explosion of wrath and abuse which it caused. He could not get the play staged, and the Church Department used its influence to procure the refusal of Ibsen's application for a Poet's grant on the Civil List. He continued to live with his wife and son in almost absolute penury. His next work, the *Pretenders*, a play with a romantic and patriotic theme, was comparatively successful, but he was ill, and the disappointment he felt at the refusal of the Norwegian government at this time to support the Danes against the German attack upon Slesvig-Holstein prevented him from taking any pleasure in his success.

In the last paragraph I spoke of 'youthful' idealism. In point of fact Ibsen, when he wrote *Love's Comedy*, was thirty-four. The fact is significant; the play is preeminently a young man's work, though the author's youth was past. In some ways Ibsen, though he lived to be old, was never to grow up. With a powerful intellect, single-minded devotion to his art, great creative zest and immense technical ability, he remained, in an odd way, spiritually immature. Advancing years did not ripen, but only hardened him; for having made the 'great refusal', he could not but find vast areas of human experience a closed book to him; the deathly aridity of his latest work, those granite monoliths of frustration and despair, is the proof of this.

Ibsen was a poet before he was a playwright, and his

early plays, with the exception of the *Pretenders*, were written in verse. He was writing poetry all through these difficult years in Bergen and Oslo. Of the quality of his poetry I cannot speak, as I do not know the Norse language, and the *soul* of poetry (if the word is not too fanciful) can never survive translation. The same, of course, is unfortunately true of prose, though in a much less degree. That Ibsen was a master of language in both mediums all who can read him in the original attest. All I can do myself by way of comment on his poetry is to indicate certain themes which occur in it and have a bearing upon the later prose plays on which his European reputation chiefly rests. That he had that snailhorn sensibility characteristic of most poets cannot be doubted, any more than the fact that it was habitually directed inward, upon himself. In one poem he describes the cruel training of a dancing bear—how the poor brute was made to stand in a heated copper while a jig was played to it; then, ever afterwards, when it heard the tune of the jig, it remembered the pain—and danced. Having told the tale, Ibsen turns it to an image of himself: 'I, too, have stood in a heated copper. . . .' Perhaps the most revealing of the poems—before he wrote the great poetic dramas *Brand* and *Peer Gynt*—is one called *On the Vidda*, a narrative poem of renunciation and in a sense of escape. The story is of a man who is lured by a strange Hunter to leave his lover and live on the mountain heights alone; gradually he conquers his grief at the half willing, half reluctant desertion, until it finally expires and leaves him 'free' to live on the heights, his heart turned to stone, while he looks down with contempt upon the emotional involvements of the misguided dwellers in the valley. It is said to be a powerful poem, but the experience out of which it is written is, to say the least, inimical to life. 'To write poetry,' Ibsen declared, 'is to hold a doom-session over oneself.' It was truly said.

At the age of thirty-six Ibsen had still failed to achieve his ambition of being recognized as Norway's national poet. He was still more or less neglected, still an outcast. He believed in poetry and in his own poetic vocation, and he believed that the revival of a great native poetry would help to lead his country to recover something of her old nobility and to arrest the creeping paralysis which he felt was destroying her social and national life. In such a revival he still hoped to be the leader, until the hope was finally crushed by the event I have already mentioned, the defeat of the Danes by the Prussians at the siege of Dybbol in 1864. Ibsen, who had dreamed not only of a united Norway but of a united Scandinavia, had done all he could to urge his country to send help to the Danes. When the Norwegian government continued to refuse, young Norwegians in considerable numbers went as volunteers, and Ibsen, saluting their patriotism and courage, called for more and ever more to join their ranks. He did not, however, volunteer himself, and when an acquaintance rashly asked him the reason, he contented himself with the reply: 'We poets have other tasks.' Ibsen had not the happy gift of courage: in Grimstad once he was proffering his heart to a young lady of some social pretensions, when her father appeared upon the scene. Ibsen fled, leaving his love to face her parent's wrath alone.

Norway's failure over the affair of Slesvig-Holstein was to Ibsen a crushing blow. She had now failed not only him but also, in Ibsen's view, herself, and he decided to turn his back upon her for ever. With the aid of a small grant of money from the public funds he left, with his wife and child, for the South. Save for one brief visit he was not to return to Norway for twenty-seven years—when he came as a European celebrity in frock-coat and top-hat, admired, respected, rich, but more profoundly miserable than ever.

This melancholy story is not agreeable reading, but it is necessary to tell it if one is to make a fair assessment of the work by which Ibsen, outside Norway, is chiefly remembered. Many people in this country, after the tremendous impact of *The Doll's House* and *Ghosts*, besides paying homage to the technical genius of the playwright, looked upon Ibsen as a great thinker and social reformer. It is true, indeed, that he was acutely aware of certain pretences upon which contemporary society was founded, and wished them away: the loveless marriage, for instance, which the subjection of wives to their husbands and the avoidance of 'questioning which probes to endless dole' dress up in the outward appearance of a stable union; but he was never, in the proper sense of the word, a thinker. He dealt not in ideas but in visions. A poet first, a poet he remained even after he had abandoned poetry for prose, and a poet's task, as he himself said is *to see*. What Ibsen saw, or came to see, sometimes with frightful clarity, was the arctic desolation of his own spirit, and his latest plays were all extended metaphors to suggest or express that vision. No one who fails to understand this can read Ibsen aright. Even his desire for social reform was built upon shaky foundations, if he meant what he said in a letter to a friend, declaring that a social conscience was nothing but a burden to a man and that there were times when the whole history of the world seemed to him a vast shipwreck, while the one thing worth doing was to save oneself. Evidently he had failed to learn from the New Testament that such a thing is psychologically impossible.

The first fruit of Ibsen's stay in the South was the verse drama *Brand*, which he wrote in Rome, dreaming of the mountains and fiords and high fells of his native Norway from which he was an exile. Like *On the Vidda, Brand* is a drama of renunciation, informed by the terrible inhuman doctrine of 'All or Nothing', as dear to Ibsen the artist as it was to the Danish philosopher Kierkegaard, with whom his spirit shared much. Pastor Brand is furiously impelled to refuse all compromise; to save his own soul he sacrifices his wife, his child and his parishioners and all that makes life warm and dear to other men. Certain saints of the Christian Church pursued, one reads, a similar path, hanging themselves from hooks, sitting on pillars, or festering in the Syrian desert. It has never seemed to me a fruitful policy—but one can only wonder at the variety of human experience, and abstain from judgement. Brand, Ibsen said, was the nobler part of his own nature. The poem—it was not primarily intended for the stage, though it was acted quite recently in London—has much of the bleak grandeur of the Norwegian mountains, a primitive strength, harsh, irresistible and dark. In Norway it made Ibsen's name; from the moment of its appearance he was accepted, at last, as the national poet.

Brand was quickly followed by another verse drama, better known to English readers and play-goers, *Peer*

Gynt. *Peer Gynt* is an altogether more humane and attractive work than its gaunt predecessor, and much of its lightness and fantasy, as well as its fundamental seriousness, survives in the English translations. Ibsen's countrymen hailed it with a mixture of delight and resentment: delight for the verve with which the dream-like incidents, pure embodiments of fantasy and Norse legend, are presented, and resentment at recognizing in the irresponsible character of Peer a satirical portrait of their own national character. The theme of the play is again a man's search for his soul, but the tone and treatment are, for Ibsen, unique. Ibsen, for once, has taken a holiday from despair, and allowed himself to look at the variety of life with a certain amused detachment. For the moment his own being is no longer its agonized centre. Not without truth Ibsen makes Peer 'find himself' at the end of the play, after his adventures amongst the cow-girls and the trolls, the lunatics, the business men and the wild dwellers in the desert, in his return to the faithful Solveig, who has grown old in her mountain hut and not forgotten him. Peer's cry, 'My mother—and my wife!' perhaps strikes a discordant note; but a touch of sentimentality, in Ibsen of all men, must not be taken too hard, though in point of fact mothers and wives are better not confused.

His reputation made by these two verse dramas and his days of poverty over, Ibsen wrote no more poetry. With a single-minded intensity of purpose he turned to prose drama instead. None the less, he remained essentially a poet and the prose plays arose from the same springs of cold fire as the poetry had done. Though *Brand* and *Peer Gynt* had established him as Norway's leading man of letters, it was the next three plays which made him the most admired, the most hated and the most discussed writer in Europe. The period which gives him his title to appear in this book had begun.

The second of these plays, *A Doll's House*, is simply as 'theatre' a brilliant piece of work, and as an essay in social criticism it was both valid and courageous. I say 'was', because the particular social attitude which it was designed to expose for reprobation has vanished from the modern world. Women are no longer dolls or toys, but are admitted (as they were in Shakespeare's, and even in Molière's, day) to be persons and to enjoy a moral equality with men. 'Shakespeare,' Shaw wrote in his *Quintessence of Ibsenism*, 'had put ourselves on the stage and not our situations. Ibsen supplies the want left by Shakespeare. He gives us not only ourselves but our situations. The things that happen to his stage figures happen to us . . . One consequence is that they are capable both of hurting us cruelly and of filling us with excited hopes of escape from idealistic tyrannies and with visions of intenser life in the future.' That comment of Bernard Shaw's well expresses the impact of this play upon the more perceptive British public of the latter end of the century. It was the theme that counted; the play pulled no punches; it dealt openly and boldly with a very real abuse, a maggot in the core of social convention, eating out the sap of family life. In an age when the drama in general was divorced from reality this step forward into 'realism'—into the treatment of a human situation which was common and recognizable but almost universally hushed up by tacit consent—this ruthless exposure of a lie at the heart of the most sacred of social institutions, marriage, was an incomparable service to the drama as a whole. At one blow it brought it back to where it had formerly been and from whence it had strayed into all sorts of sentimental absurdities and melodramatic nonsense. It gave to European drama the chance to become again what it used to be, a high and serious art, by linking it once more with the real passions of men and women. This alone, even apart from the intrinsic quality of the plays of this period, would put Ibsen amongst the great European playwrights. The plays, however, are also constructed with a meticulous and sensitive art, especially, perhaps, *A Doll's House. A Doll's House* has a formal perfection new to the stage in Ibsen's day. It is as logical as Euclid, as coherent as the molecules in a lump of matter. Not a word is wasted or inert, and only at the end, when Nora tells her husband that she is going to leave him, do we realize how every small incident, every speech, every metaphor almost, throughout the course of the play has prepared us for the inevitable denouement. By a hundred hints and suggestions we are made, by an almost uncanny skill, to participate in the Helmers' dozen years of married life, to sense their essential aridity, to feel the first rumblings of the earthquake which is to lay in ruin that building so seemly to the eye, so that when the shock comes it comes without surprise. This is the high art of dramatic technique—the artifice, perhaps, if the word can be used without derogatory intent. There are other ways to write good drama, but this conscious artistry with its ruthless rejection of the irrelevant fashions its own formal beauty, and deserves the admiration which we owe to everything perfect in its kind. *A Doll's House* is greatly superior to its predecessor *The Pillars of Society*, which was the first of Ibsen's 'social' dramas; its theme, the exposure of commercial dishonesty in the wealthy bourgeois families of a small Norwegian town (it was Grimstad which Ibsen had in mind), was a hard-hitting tract for the times and relevant by no means only in Norway, but a modern British audience is apt to find the play over-contrived, lacking in characterization and somewhat woodenly melodramatic in the turns of the plot. One doesn't want the moral tub, even if it is a good tub, thumped too hard on the stage, or indeed in any art; this tub was undoubtedly a good one, being concerned in particular with the hideous practice amongst ship-owners of sending rotten ships to sea in order to collect the insurance money. Two years before the play was written, in 1875, Samuel Plimsoll, after a great struggle, had got the House of Commons to bring in new legislation to stop this abuse.

Art has no rules. In art everything is legitimate, provided that it succeeds. *A Doll's House* did succeed, triumphantly; but it is worth noting that in both these plays—*A Doll's House* and *Pillars of Society*—Ibsen was running, as an artist, a grave risk. He was using the stage as a pulpit. Now all great art has lessons for us as well as delight, but we learn those lessons, so to speak, unawares, much as we learn from certain people who we know are good though they never instruct us how to behave. Ibsen, at this important period when he was writing his 'social' plays, consciously assumed the office of instructor. He was no longer an angry young man: he was an angry middle-aged one, and, as angry men of any age are bound to be, bitterly at odds both with society and himself. Like all serious people, he was concerned with how life should be lived, personally and socially. He was acutely aware of the façade which society presents to hide its sins, and passionately eager to tear it down. He was for truth at all costs—a perilous aim, for nobody knows precisely in what truth consists; for him there must be no illusion, no pretence, no comfortable concealment of harsh realities, no compromise with the devil, or the old Adam in man. He wanted to make his contemporaries, especially his own countrymen whom he both loved and hated, see once and for all the falsehoods upon which their public life was founded, the hidden lies, the grub at the root of their social conventions. What was the Helmers' marriage *really* like? What sort of person, under his mask of respectability, was Counsellor Bernick, whom everyone looked up to as a pillar of society? Ibsen was not much interested in politics as such; he refused to identify himself with a party. For him there were no palliatives for the sick society he saw; he wanted revolution, but it must be a revolution within the spirit of man. Contemptible mankind, he felt, must change its nature, or be damned. It was a tall order.

In his personal life Ibsen's demand took a similar form: what he groped after was 'freedom and truth'—two noble ideals if only one can give them a vital content. He was determined at all costs to 'be himself', to realize his own nature, to get rid of all pretences and shackles which might obscure or bind what he felt to be the innermost essence of his individual being. Nine-tenths of life, he told himself, was lies and slavery; his task, and the task of all great men, was to see the lies for what they were and to break the enslaving bonds. A man's true happiness he saw as freedom from all restraint, either from within or from without, the right to be himself, to exercise all his powers in perfect freedom, responsible to none. Well, Satan, in *Paradise Lost* had precisely the same views, and we know where they got him. It is hard to write of these things, but some attempt, I think, must be made to understand them if we are to see Ibsen in his proper place in the literature of the world, and not only as the English 'Ibsenites', such men as Archer, Gosse and Shaw, saw him at the end of last century. These men saw him as the liberator, as the mighty playwright (which indeed he was) who let a gale of fresh air into the musty conventions of the contemporary theatre and dared to speak of forbidden subjects which lay at the very heart of civilised life. They saw him as the lonely idealist crying out for liberty and truth—and cry for liberty and truth Ibsen most assuredly did; but what, in fact, did those noble abstractions become on the lips which proclaimed them? The liberty that Ibsen longed for became a monstrous egotism; he thought to 'find himself' by severing ties, rejecting responsibilities, cutting out dependencies, narrowing the wide ambience of life to the small, hard core of his individual being—as if a rose were to quarrel with its roots and the earth they are buried in, and the rain that moistens the earth and the clouds which bring the rain; and the truth which Ibsen sought turned out, in the end, to be the dust and ashes of despair. This must be remembered in any final assessment of Ibsen, or when we place him in our minds beside some of the other men I have written of in this book; but it need not blind us to his power, or to the restless energy of thought, the dedicated purpose, the passionate persistence with which in his social dramas he brought upon the stage (the most instant and irresistible of all means of communication) the new ideas which elsewhere in Europe, in the work of such men as Mill, Spencer, Darwin, Marx, or the destructive Biblical criticism of Strauss, were already abroad and disturbing men's minds with thoughts 'beyond the reaches of their souls'. In the latter half of the nineteenth century there were many catfish in the bowl of received opinions. Ibsen was not the least active of them.

Pillars of Society had its gleams of hope for the poor midget which is man; so had *A Doll's House*, in that Nora, as the curtain comes down, allows us to fancy that somehow, some time, the 'miracle might happen'; but in the next play, *Ghosts*, all the gleams are extinguished. There is utter darkness. In his own battle for spiritual and intellectual freedom Ibsen was becoming more and more aware that the barriers against it consisted not only in the weight of convention and the innumerable petty claims which life in society make upon a man but also in the compulsive and accumulating pressures of the past. He had discovered, not without anguish, that we are the sons of our fathers—and even the descendants of Adam and the apes. It was these pressures from the past which he called the Ghosts, haunting us, and allowing us no hope of escape. In the play he gives his thought a frightful emphasis by narrowing it down to its purely biological aspect: Osvald, longing for life, is doomed to madness and death by a malady inherited from his father, who contracted it as a result of loose living. This disagreeable fact, though the hinge on which *Ghosts* is hung, is yet in a sense only a symbol of a greater horror; the apostle of freedom has discovered that our lives are predetermined by an inescapable necessity.

The publication of *Ghosts* caused a hubbub in Norway, not so much by its philosophical implications as by the open reference to a hitherto unmentionable disease. In all the reviews Ibsen was violently attacked, and he responded by writing *An Enemy of the People*, which, save for parts of *Peer Gynt*, was the only amusing play, in spite of its slightly acid flavour, he ever produced. His Doctor Stockmann is an enemy of the people of his town because he dared to expose the unfortunate fact that the baths, upon which the prosperity of the town was founded, were infected by waste from the tannery. Like Ibsen himself, he told the 'truth', and the truth was unpalatable. *Ghosts* in some of the reviews had been compared with the muck-raking realism of Zola: 'Zola', Ibsen replied, 'goes down into the sewer to take a bath; I, to clean it out.' He was determined at any rate to maintain the purity of his intentions.

An Enemy of the People was the last of the social plays. After it, Ibsen turned from the criticism of society to what had always been his primary concern, the agonized and brooding study of the condition and conscience of the individual—that is, of himself. The result was a succession of plays of unprecedented power but hardly more heartening in their effect upon audience or reader. But before the great series began, there was a curious play, very important in any study of Ibsen, about which a word must be said. This play was *The Wild Duck*.

Ibsen, as I have already suggested, was no philosopher. Ideas he had in plenty: he flung them out in all directions as a rocket its stars; but he made no attempt to combine them, except, in the end, in a blank negation. Usually the ideas had been ideals of some kind—

the 'no compromise' of Pastor Brand, the perfect marriage glimpsed in imagination by Nora Helmer, the hope of a society based on honest dealing instead of self-interest. The refusal of compromise between the claims of ordinary life and the life of the artist as he imagined it, Ibsen had tried to enforce in his own practice, withdrawing himself deeper and deeper into the cavern of his own individuality. The attempt had not brought him happiness; and now, suddenly, he looked at the problem afresh. Might it not be that the reiterated claims of the ideal, far from raising humanity to a nobler existence, acted in fact as a toxic to destroy the agreeable illusions upon which nearly all men and women do, and must, rely if life is to be tolerable? Consequently in *The Wild Duck* he told the story of young Gregers Werle and his attempt to bring the light of truth into the family of his friend Hjalmar Ekdal, a weak creature only fit to live upon dreams. Werle, with his ruthless idealism, is as stupid as an ox, and the result of his exposure of the background of his friend's history, which he is in a position to know, is of course disastrous. Hjalmar's daughter, a child of fifteen, is driven in despair to shoot herself. So there we have it—we cannot live, it seems, either with lies or without them. Heads I win, says the Devil, tails you lose. Yet in this play too, as in all the prose plays, Ibsen the craftsman is beyond compare; he makes his audience believe in those dreary figures—though the dice are so loaded against them that in other hands they would be incredible. He holds our attention to the end, to the last depressing bang of the pistol-shot in the attic. He does it by sheer theatrical expertise, and by the wonderfully natural quality of his dialogue—a quality one can guess at in the translations and to which all those who can read him in his own language bear witness.

After *The Wild Duck*, Ibsen, in 1885, revisited Norway. He was famous now, and made much of by his countrymen. But a few months sickened him of his home, and he hurried back to Germany, where he had lived on and off for years. His relationship with his own people was curious and interesting, a compound of resentful hostility and a longing to be admired and loved. He was a Norseman to the bone, but with his fellow Norsemen he found it impossible to live. Not that he found it easier to live with Germans or Italians, for in Rome or Munich or Berchtesgaden he would see no-one, but shut himself up in solitude—and dream of the Norwegian sea and the Norwegian mountains. All his plays have a Norwegian setting, except one. He was to be an exile for six more years.

Meanwhile the final series of plays, tremendous dramas of ever deepening and darkening self-knowledge, was begun—*Rosmersholm*, *Hedda Gabler*, *The Master Builder*, *Little Eyolf*, *John Gabriel Borkman*. It would be tedious, I think, to consider here each of these plays in detail, so I will confine myself to some general reflections.

Ibsen was growing old. He was less combative than he used to be. His anger against the follies of society was dying down: he was tired of playing catfish in the bowl. Once an acquaintance had expressed surprise that Ibsen the apostle of freedom and individuality should oppose the abolition of corporal punishment in schools. 'What,' he asked, 'would you like your son Sigurd to be whipped?' 'No,' Ibsen replied, 'I should like him to whip.' It was a revelatory answer. But now he no longer felt the need of the lash. He was still an angry man, but the anger was turning more and more inward. The final triumph of Ibsen's art was to be the revelation of his own spiritual failure.

In these last plays Ibsen is no longer concerned with men in their social relationships; his interest is concentrated upon the individual consciousness, locked away in its own secrecy and solitude. Passionate devotee, as he had always been, of 'truth', he now set himself to probe the hidden springs of action in his own heart and to give his findings imaginative expression in his work. All the plays are, in their different ways, revelations of what Plato called 'the lie in the soul', which, traced back through a complex of human relationships or unravelled from a tangled thread of dreams, ultimately and inevitably lays a life in ruin. Technically the plays are as unique as they are masterly: outwardly, little happens; there is a minimum of action in the ordinary sense. Each play opens with the chief character or characters standing as it were on the edge of a precipice, of the proximity of which they are only dimly aware, and towards which they are impelled by the progressive realization of the true significance of the past. Piecemeal and relentlessly, by sudden questions, chance words, unexpected glimpses, the cross-lights of imaginative reflexion, the discovery or re-discovery of some suppressed or forgotten fact, the apparition of some still unexorcised ghost, the nature of the lie in the soul is revealed and demands to be confronted. The precipice is there—waiting. The life of the Rosmers 'ennobles, but it kills joy'; and John Rosmer (in *Rosmersholm*), when Rebecca finally under his influence admits the fearful truth, knows that, though he loves her, he can trust her only in death; Borkman (in *John Gabriel Borkman*) who has lived under the illusion of a frustrated genius is brought in the end to confront his almost forgotten betrayal of life and love when he married the rich sister instead of the one who loved him, and thus is driven to meet the icy blast from the fells which is at once the symbol and the material cause of his death; Solness (in *The Master Builder*) has tried to conceal from himself his ruthless egotism by constructing a personal myth of his possession by demonic powers, and is brought to ruin by the one person he knows who dares to challenge him to make good his claim. Each play is haunted by its ghosts: the white horses of the house of Rosmer, where no-one, as the servant said, was ever heard to laugh; Borkman's loveless marriage and the years in prison; the struggles and frustrations of Solness' youth, to escape from which he was impelled to build up over the years the false legend of his genius. They are ghosts from the past, yet stalk, by Ibsen's incomparable art, through the present, filling it with a knowledge of inevitable doom—as the ghost of that one fateful moment of blind passion haunts the life of the Allmers in *Little Eyolf*. It is a drama of ever deepening psychological insight, which nevertheless as it deepens, narrows, until it seems to be concentrated upon a single point, like a neuralgic pain. All these later plays are extended metaphors of Ibsen's own personal consciousness—hugely extended and rich in imaginative invention, but all welling up from the same bitter spring. 'I never describe a situation,' Ibsen had said long before, 'which I have not lived through.' It was true when he said it, but now, in his latest period, it had a more piercing truth. 'Look into your heart,' said Raleigh, and write; Ibsen looked into his heart, and out of the desolation he found there, he wrote these plays. There were moments of respite, as when, for instance, he wrote *The Lady from the Sea*, a play which so curiously anticipates some of the findings of modern mind-therapy, in that Ellida, the wife, is made to free herself from her obsession with a half-imaginary lover by being forced by her husband to confront the actuality and to make her choice in absolute freedom. But *The Lady from the Sea* was only an interlude in the terrible series of self-questioning in plays where the leading characters—Hedda, Solness, Borkman, Rubek—come nearer and nearer to madness. The plays baffled his countrymen, as they baffled the English Ibsenites, who were quick enough to seize with delight upon Ibsen's earlier, savage adventures in sociology or iconoclasm; but this was something different, and strange. All sorts of irrelevant interpretations were put upon the plays, as if they still trafficked in 'ideas' and Ibsen were still the social critic and satirist. But these plays did nothing of the kind, and Ibsen was no longer interested in society. He was concerned solely with himself.

After *John Gabriel Borkman* there was one more play, *When We Dead Awaken*, and more than all the others it was a vision of his own dereliction and despair. 'It is his own life problem,' wrote his compatriot and biographer Koht, who knew him better than anyone else did, 'that trembles and vibrates through the play, almost without concealment or change.' Throughout this chapter I have hinted at what this problem was. Ibsen wanted freedom to be himself. The phrase has a gallant sound, an adventurous ring; but anyone who demands freedom to be himself cannot but come in the end to the realization of what, precisely, that self is. There are two, or more, men in all of us; Ibsen was no exception. He wanted life—whatever that means—or thought he wanted it: he wanted to do deeds, to control the destinies of men, to fight, to love; to drink, like Ulysses, life to the lees. And he also wanted to be a poet. For him the two things appeared to conflict—the life of action and human companionship, the 'lovely earth-life' as he makes Irene call it in his last play, and the life of imagination. He chose the life of imagination, dedicated himself to it utterly and ruthlessly, and found, in doing so, that the other, real life had passed him by. He had never 'lived' at all. He had been 'only' a poet. 'I was born to be an artist,' he makes the sculptor Rubek say, 'and, do what I may, I shall never be anything else. When we dead awaken, what do we really see? We see that we have never lived.'

That was the Epilogue which Ibsen wrote upon his life's work.

Of course it is not really true to say that Ibsen deliberately 'chose' the artist's life and deliberately rejected the other. Human nature does not work like that. Ibsen was what he was, for better or worse, and, like the rest of us, he had perforce to deal with the material he was born with. But, being an artist, he was acutely conscious of the conflict within himself, between—to put it baldly—what he was and what he would have liked to be. No one knew better than he that he had let life go by, and no-one ever suffered more bitterly for the knowledge. The suffering is stamped upon all he wrote once he had come to maturity—the suffering and the resentment. Ibsen knew that he lacked courage; reminded in middle age of how he had run away from the angry father of his lady-love in Grimstad, 'Yes,' he said ruefully, 'I have never been brave *face to face.*' He was afraid of heights (like Solness in the *Master Builder*), and of being exposed to possible infection when he was abroad. He was afraid of joining the volunteers to fight the Germans at Dybbol; he was afraid, one may guess, of love. The 'lovely earth-life' he longed for was a dangerous business, and his nature impelled him to shun it. The old lion had, in fact, a timorous heart. The same shrinking, the same lack of confidence, is reflected in his inability to take hostile criticism; the least breath of it put him in a rage. His friend Björnsen having written an enthusiastic review of *Peer Gynt*, Ibsen wrote him a letter of warm thanks; but, when almost immediately afterwards a hostile notice appeared in another paper with which Björnsen had connections, Ibsen at once suspected his friend, quite wrongly, of having inspired it—and did not send his letter. Perhaps the lack of confidence had further expression in Ibsen's determined hunt for decorations and public honours of all kinds, and in the meticulously careful management of his financial affairs. He never forgot the apothecary's apprentice and the old humiliations.

In 1891 Ibsen returned to Norway for good and settled in Oslo. He was now a world-figure and Norway was proud of him. He took little or no part in public or social life, but shut himself up to brood and dream. Every day at the same hour he took his walk in top hat and frock coat down Karl Johan street to his café, where his table was reserved. His son Sigurd had done well in the foreign service, and his wife was still with him but there was little communion between them: they were 'two lonely old people', as a contemporary described them. There in Oslo his last four plays were written. In the spring of 1900 he had a stroke, which was repeated the following year and partially paralysed him. His son found him one day with a sheet of paper before him; 'Look,' he said, 'here am I trying to form the letters of the alphabet—I, who was once an author.' Some strength he regained, and was able for a few more years to take drives with his physician in sledge or carriage. He died on May 23, 1906, and was given a State funeral with public mourning. He was seventy-eight years old. On his seventieth birthday he had received hundreds of congratulatory telegrams from all over the world, and it is, I think, both touching and significant that the one he valued most was from Nansen, that man of self-regardless action and indomitable courage, who had only recently returned from his adventures in the Polar ice.

Ibsen was a great playwright not only by reason of the intrinsic power and brilliance of his work, but also because he opened new territories which the drama could explore. In his middle period, the period of the social plays, he revivified the art of drama by the 'naturalism' which allowed his characters to express themselves in the real language of men, the actual contemporary speech—much as Dickens did in his novels —and by the 'realism' which brought upon the stage matters of intimate and vital concern to all intelligent men and women. But that he was not amongst the very greatest should be clear from what I have already written. If the highest art, the art of such men as Shakespeare, Sophocles, Molière, Beethoven, is, as I believe it to be, something by which we live, then Ibsen falls short of it. He falls short of it because all his work was written out of anger, or resentment, or despair. Anger, resentment and despair are negative passions; Ibsen never came to terms with life or grew to a real spiritual maturity. He had made what Dante in a different context called *il gran rifiuto*, the great refusal. Hence, behind all he saw with such penetrating insight, such frightful clarity, one is aware of what he did *not* see—what Shakespeare, for instance, never lost sight of even in his moments of blackest anguish. Ibsen, the apostle of truth, told the great lie, in that in his latest work he narrowed life down to a single needle-point of pain. He lacked Faith: faith in God, faith in man, and, most of all, faith in himself. That is why his work, so tremendous in its impact on his contemporaries and still holding the fascination of all dark things, has, to take it as a whole, little to give to us today. There is the touch of death in it—like the Ice Chapel to which Pastor Brand came amongst the Norwegian fells.

Mansell Collection

IBSEN

From the portrait by W. Pech

Radio Times Hulton Picture Library

SHAW

V

GEORGE BERNARD SHAW
1856–1950

SHAW'S last joke—and he made many during his life of more than ninety years—was to leave the bulk of his large fortune to a project for the improvement of English spelling. He was nothing if not unpredictable. Now I intend no injustice to Shaw by this remark. He was a towering figure in English letters, and underneath the incessant pyrotechnic display of verbal wit and paradox which makes his long series of comedies the most dazzling in the history of the modern stage, he had a profoundly serious intellectual purpose. That the purpose was intellectual rather than artistic, though his artistry was often superb, is the key to understanding him.

In the Dedicatory Letter to *Man and Superman* Shaw has told us what he himself chiefly sought and admired in literature: this was, he declared, an explicit and reasoned philosophy of life. In his estimation both Shakespeare and Dickens, whose work he read constantly and with pleasure, fell short in this particular. Neither of them had a philosophy of life; each was so much concerned with particulars that he was blind to principles. Neither could see the wood for the trees—and it is the wood that counts, however impressive the trees, in their isolated and individual being, may appear. Shakespeare and Dickens, in short, lacked ideas;

'in all their fictions,' Shaw wrote, 'there is no leading thought or inspiration for which any man could conceivably risk the spoiling of his hat in a shower, much less his life;' while to Shakespeare the world was merely a stage of fools on which he himself was utterly bewildered—'he could see no sort of sense in living at all'. John Bunyan, on the contrary, having a recognizable and valid philosophy of life, was, in Shaw's view and in virtue of that fact, the greater writer. The famous Allegory, which Shaw described as a consistent attack on conventional morality and respectability, revealed Bunyan's sense of the only true joy in life, the being used for a purpose recognized by himself as a mighty one—'the being a force of Nature instead of a feverish little selfish clod of ailments and grievances complaining that the world will not devote itself to making you happy.'

Shaw was always fond of overstating his case, but from these remarks of his about Shakespeare and Bunyan it is not difficult to guess at his own aims as a dramatic writer, and at the conception he formed of the place he wished to occupy in the literature of the stage. Indeed, there is no need to guess; for he has told us, often and categorically, as was his way. 'I must warn the reader,' he wrote in the preface to the collection of his dramatic criticisms, 'that what he is about to study is . . . a siege laid to the theatre of the XIXth century by an author who had to cut his own way into it at the point of the pen, and throw some of its defenders into the moat. I postulated as desirable a certain kind of play in which I was destined ten years later to make my mark as a playwright; and I brought everybody, authors, actors, managers, to the one test: were they coming my way or staying in the old grooves? I set up my own standard of what the drama should be and how it should be presented, and I used all my art to make every deviation in aiming at this standard seem ridiculous and old-fashioned.' The standard was the standard already set up by the social dramas of Ibsen, whom Shaw, with his life-long friend William Archer, was amongst the first people in England to recognize as the modern master. As for Ibsen in the period of *A Doll's House*, *Pillars of Society* and *An Enemy of the People*, so for Shaw throughout his long career as a playwright the function of the drama was not merely, or even primarily, to entertain but to make people think; not to provide an escape from reality into fantasy or romance, but to face an audience with facts; to strip bare a faded or tawdry idealism, to pierce the half-truths and comfortable conventions which we use as a protective screen against a too painful clarity of vision and to bring us up sharply against the real motives which actuate us. Shaw's drama was a drama of ideas; he used the stage as a debating platform and a pulpit to instruct and edify his audiences—and also as need hardly be said, to amuse them, for he was too intelligent a man not to know that a flat speech gains no votes, and a dull sermon saves no souls. Shaw's speeches were far from flat and his homilies far from dull; on the contrary, all his determined attempts to expose the congenital idiocy of practically everyone in the world except himself (with Ibsen, Shelley, Nietszche and Sidney Webb as runners-up) are accompanied by such incandescent verbal rocketry and impudently delightful paradox that one is almost dazzled into believing them true—even when he tries to make us believe that Nelson was a typical Englishman and the dour Duke of Wellington a typical Irishman. Shaw made war upon illusions: upon the illusions of power, wealth, class and opportunity on which, he thought, society is built, upon the illusions of morality which regulate and stultify the relationship between the sexes, upon the illusions of mere mindlessness which determine people's attitude to religion. He hated and despised what he called 'romantic morality' and professed to trace the failure of the modern world to the attempt to found our institutions on 'the ideals suggested to our imaginations by our half-satisfied passions instead of on a genuinely scientific natural history'. In all this Shaw was passionately sincere; though his method, with its almost impish iconoclasm, its sustained topsy-turveydom (Max Beerbohm's cartoon represented him as standing on his head) was often the method of deliberate showmanship, he was genuinely concerned with making a better world. Whether the world he envisaged would in fact have been an improvement on the one we know, is open to doubt; for it may well be that for beings created, as we are, to see through a glass darkly, a certain admixture of illusion, if by that we mean those intimations which have no logical foundation and cannot be explained or pigeonholed by the intellect alone, is a necessary and precious element in what we conceive to be the truth of things. Intellectual passion—which was the only passion Shaw recognized as a noble one—is noble indeed; but it is as well to realize that the dry light of the unaided intellect is an insufficient guide through the changes and chances of this sublunary world. The state of the Ancients in Shaw's *Back to Methuselah*, if it is taken as anything more than an amusing fantasy to remind us that seventy years is all too brief a span to learn wisdom in, is as frightful an imagining as any I can remember in literature. It is significant that of all the great Romantic poets the only one whom Shaw admired was Shelley—and that, not for his poetry for which he cared not at all, but for his ideas about religion and society, especially as Shelley expressed them in his boyish poem *Queen Mab*. These limitations, for limitations they are, help to explain, to me at any rate, why Shaw bequeathed his money to an alphabet rather than to his friends, of whom he had many. None the less he was a great playwright: he invented a new kind of drama for the English stage and, when nobody liked it, continued with immense courage and persistence until he had forced audiences in Britain, Europe and America to recognize its quality. Shaw made us laugh and he made us think, and each was an inestimable service. He made us laugh because he knew his job as a writer of comedy, and he made us think because his themes were all fundamentally serious and important; however mistaken he may have been, and often was, he had a deep and genuine concern for the moral and physical welfare of humanity. He liked to consider himself a religious writer, and no doubt he was entitled to his opinion. In the terrestrial heaven he envisaged there would have been no poverty, no sin, and little joy.

George Bernard Shaw, who came of an Irish Protestant family was born in Dublin in 1856. Amongst his ancestors were a number of able men, distinguished in politics and finance, but his grandfather, a solicitor and stockbroker, lost his fortune through the fraudulence of a partner. George Carr Shaw, the playwright's father, was twelve years old when the disaster happened. He grew up in poverty and showed no sign of either the will or the ability to improve his circumstances. Through the influence of a relative he obtained a sinecure in the Dublin Law Courts, but the post was soon abolished and he was awarded a pension of £60 a year. The pension was commuted for a lump sum of £500, which he invested in a corn mill, a wholesale business which just, but only just, supported him. When he was thirty-seven he married. The future playwright was the only son and third child of the marriage.

Shaw's childhood was not a happy one. His father was incompetent, feckless and a drunkard; his mother, who supplemented the family income by teaching singing, was a frigid woman who despised her husband and had little or no love for her children. Her maternal feeling, in so far as she had any, was concentrated upon the elder daughter, who, it was hoped, would become an opera singer; of the extraordinary ability and promise of her son she had not the slightest inkling. For the boy Shaw it was a chilly childhood, destitute of love, the one essential thing for the health of any family, rich or poor, distinguished or obscure. Taught in various inconspicuous schools, Shaw worked with moderate diligence, and, as he grew older, gained for himself a knowledge of art by frequenting the picture-galleries of Dublin and laid the foundations of the wide and intimate knowledge of music which was to serve him well and delight him continually in the years to come. Sensitive and affectionate by nature he had a fund of human kindliness which circumstances forbade him to express: his mother is said to have disliked being touched; his father's weakness filled him with shame and disgust—in revulsion he himself became a teetotaller and remained so throughout his life. It was an arid childhood for a boy who wanted affection, and knew, moreover, that he had more than his share of intelligence, though not one of his own people appreciated the fact or was even aware of it. He was early forced to grow a protective shell from which, as usually happens, he never wholly emerged: in later life it took the form of a certain apparent hardness towards other people's distress and of a tendency, which his enemies have been quick to denounce, to self-advertisement by the flaunting of his idiosyncrasies both of habit and opinion, and of the pursuit of paradox for the sake of paradox rather than for the sake of truth. No man is more combative than the man who is unsure. He was capable of the greatest generosity, and from all the weaknesses of the flesh he was, as boy and man, singularly free.

When Shaw was sixteen his mother left Dublin and went with her daughters to live in London, to continue to profit from the musical instruction of a singing-master named Lee, who had migrated thither a short time before. People thought that Mrs. Shaw was Lee's lover, but Shaw himself knew better; after her death he remarked to a friend that a man who could seduce his mother could as easily seduce the wooden Virgin at Nuremberg, and that she could have boarded the three musketeers for twenty years without discovering their sex. Shaw was now living alone with his father. A year previously he had entered the firm of a Dublin estate-agency as a junior clerk, where he quickly won promotion, and by the time his mother broke up the family he held the position of cashier and was responsible for collecting rents over a wide area. Competence in practical matters was throughout his life a component of

Shaw's variously gifted nature: he was one of the few authors who always managed his own business affairs, and managed them successfully. In this he resembled his earliest master, Ibsen.

After five years in the Dublin office Shaw, then twenty years old, resigned his post and went to join his mother in London without any clear idea of how he was to earn his living. For a long time he failed to do so, to the annoyance of his sister Lucy. One or two odd jobs came his way, amongst them writing musical criticism as Lee's 'ghost' in an obscure paper; then, after two years, he wrote his first novel. It was a failure, like its four successors. By this time he at least knew what was the work he wished, and was determined, to do; it was to be literature or nothing. The measure of his determination, once it was come to, is the extraordinary fact that he had the patience and courage to write five novels in succession without any encouragement or financial advantage. From the age of twenty Shaw was a dedicated writer, but it was many years before he found his proper form of expression. Meanwhile his mother and Lucy, who were both earning money by their music (the younger sister died just before Shaw came to London), looked upon him with disapproval as an idler and tolerated his presence in the house as a necessary nuisance. It amused him in later life to record that his earnings as a literary man for the first nine years were £6.

During this period of unprofitable literary labour—Shaw could not tell a story and would never have made a novelist—he was becoming more and more deeply engaged in politics, which, after play-writing—or even before it, as many of his plays were to be concerned directly or indirectly with political matters—was the leading passion of his life. He has himself told us that it was listening to a lecture by Henry George, an American and author of a book which advocated the Single Tax on land values as the cure of all social ills, that first converted him to socialism. Soon afterwards he began his long and close association with Sidney Webb and became, with him, a leading member of the newly founded Fabian Society, of which the chief political tenets were nationalization of the means of production and equal political rights for men and women. Both in these early years and for a long time to come Shaw worked indefatigably, and without payment, to spread the ideas of Fabian socialism, writing pamphlets, sitting on committees, speaking and lecturing in season and out of season to any society or street-corner gathering which would give him a hearing. Naturally nervous and lacking in self-confidence, he had at first to force himself to speak in public until, with practice, he discovered that he was an orator and could hold an audience for an hour or more when other speakers, at the same meeting, had been shouted down. He spoke always extempore and without notes, and, once he had discovered his power, gloried in it. He never refused an invitation to lecture, if it was in any way possible to accept it—his best political speech, he tells us in his *Sixteen Self Sketches*, was delivered in a London park, in pouring rain, to an audience of six policemen.

Novel writing was to the work which Shaw was destined to do much what learning the strokes on land is to the boy or girl who wishes to swim. In his five novels he was going through the motions of a man of letters. The next step forward towards his true vocation came through journalism—literary journalism, that is, which up to some thirty or forty years ago offered far more opportunity and scope to a lively and critical mind than it does today, when the battle for sales and solvency leaves less and less room, if indeed it leaves any at all, in the daily and evening papers for anything so interesting as humane discussion of the arts. He began by reviewing books for the *Pall Mall Gazette* and soon went on to write musical criticism for the *Star* and the *World* and dramatic criticism, under the editorship of the notorious Frank Harris, for the *Saturday Review.* Shaw's critical writing quickly made him a reputation; like everything he wrote it was witty, lively and discursive, starting all sorts of hares, linking the arts with life and society as he saw them, and serving at every opportunity his own propagandist or revolutionary purposes. Not much literary journalism retains its interest beyond the moment of its appearance, but Shaw's musical and dramatic criticism can still be read with pleasure because it was based upon a consistent sense of value and always related the ephemeral to what is permanent. On one occasion in the very early days he was asked to write a notice on some philosophical book and took six months to do it, because he found it necessary to read a dozen or more works before he felt himself qualified to express an opinion. Many modern reviewers will smile at such conscientiousness—one hopes a little uncomfortably.

It was William Archer who, observing that Shaw's novels though badly constructed and deficient in narrative skill contained nevertheless much spirited and amusing dialogue, first revealed to him his true vocation. Why, asked Archer, did Shaw not try his hand at a play? He was full of ideas, he wanted an audience, he had already perfected a clear and trenchant style, and he could write convincing dialogue. The contemporary theatre was moribund and boring; was not Shaw the man to inject new life into it? It was taken as a soporific after the day's work; could not Shaw use it to make intelligent men and women take a fresh look at certain issues, social, psychological or religious, which profoundly affected them? Why should not modern comedy, like the ancient, have an intellectual content and provoke thought as well as laughter? Not that Archer himself asked all these questions; but Shaw asked them, once the notion of playwriting was put into his head. Actually what Archer did was to suggest that he and his friend should write a play in collaboration. Shaw jumped at the suggestion, and promptly sketched out two acts. Archer however could make nothing of them, and the work was put away for seven years. Then Shaw took it out again, wrote a concluding act and offered the play, which he called *Widowers' Houses*, to the adventurous producer J. T. Grein, who in the previous year had shocked the London critics by a production of Ibsen's *Ghosts*. Shaw was thirty-six when *Widowers' Houses*, his first play, appeared upon the stage of the Royalty Theatre. It was given two performances and was then withdrawn.

In spite of this failure—and Shaw was used to failure by this time— *Widowers' Houses* made him the most talked-of playwright in London. Long notices appeared in the press, some of them abusive; one paper discussed the play and its author in an editorial. Whatever else it was, *Widowers' Houses* was something new on the London stage and of a quality impossible to ignore.

Shaw, at last, had begun his career as playwright, and in no uncertain manner.

Like Ibsen, Shaw began his work by an exposure of social abuses; but there the similarity between them ends. Shaw gave Ibsen his fervent admiration for having the courage to bring real contemporary problems upon the stage and for his refusal of mealy-mouthed romanticism. In this he was Ibsen's disciple and successor. No two men, however, could have been more different in the colour and tone of their work or in their fundamental outlook upon human affairs. One may like or dislike Ibsen; one may shrink or not, according to one's predilections, from the smoky and mephitic gloom of his later plays, but one cannot fail to recognize, and pay homage to, his power—his imaginative power. Ibsen, being a poet as well as a playwright, created a world: a world, indeed, of darkness and despair, but still a world. One can never be quite the same person again after reading or witnessing *John Gabriel Borkman* or *When we Dead Awake*, any more than one can after seeing *Hamlet* or *King Lear*. In Shaw, on the other hand, this imaginative power is absent; he was not in the true sense a creator, as were the others of whom I have written in this book, except Sheridan—though even Sheridan may be said to have created his tiny world; he was, rather, a commentator and critic who threw his comments and his criticism into brilliant and vivid dramatic form. This is in no way to belittle Shaw's work; I state the fact in order to make as clear as I can an essential difference between it and the work of the other playwrights I have discussed. It is not a question of good or bad, better or worse, but of kind; not of effect only, but of intention. All Shaw's plays are in their various ways propagandist and didactic; he has himself told us that 'for art's sake'—whatever that may mean—he would never have endured the labour of writing a single line. Poetry, and, I suppose, all great art, is, as Professor Bradley once put it, *in* the world but not *of* the world; and that seems to imply that the creative artist accepts the human condition even though it may destroy him. His business is to interpret and illuminate it. To read Shaw's plays or to see them on the stage where they belong is to be made aware of a detached and roving intellect, sharp as a knife and quick as light, combative, watching its chance to get under our guard, to upset our prejudices, expose our inconsistences, shatter our complacency, mock the futility of our blind emotional life—to teach us, in short, not to be silly. An admirable purpose, but how difficult to achieve! Shaw the playwright was a sort of archangelical schoolmaster, working on the modern principle of education through entertainment, but though all the lessons he wished to teach were of the liveliest kind and all on the side of honour, decency and truth, he had the defect of many mundane schoolmasters, in that he never really understood the hidden sources from which flowed the errors of his pupils. No poverty and a maximum of three hours work a day will not necessarily make society happy and good, and chatter about the Life Force will be unlikely to make us deal more successfully with our love affairs or be any more reasonable in our religious beliefs. To Shaw's peculiarly constituted nature, life, one feels, was a less rich and complex thing than in fact it is, and of the real passions which move mankind he remained, in an odd way, a spectator only, sometimes amused, more often irritated, and never himself involved in them.

Widowers' Houses is a telling exposure of the evil of slum landlordism. It was quickly followed By *Mrs. Warren's Profession*, in which the object of his attack is tainted money and a social economy by which girls are driven to prostitution. The play was banned. Shaw had from the first the most essential quality of the playwright, a fine feeling for stage effect: he knew instinctively what in the presentation of character, in dialogue, in the placing of his climaxes and manipulation of surprises, was properly dramatic—what, in short, would *tell*. This dramatic expertise is evident in the first of his plays, in spite of its somewhat scrambled ending; in *Mrs. Warren's Profession* it is already supreme. Many of his later plays were to break all the rules of dramatic construction, but however shapeless and wayward they were, they seldom or never failed in effectiveness: for Shaw never lost the faculty of making even talk without action dramatic and, given the right actor, could hold an audience with a packed and closely reasoned speech occupying two full pages of print.

The commercial failure of his first two plays suggested to Shaw the expedient, at that time an unfamiliar one, of publishing them in book form, together with one other 'unpleasant' play (the word was his own), *The Philanderer*. They were duly printed, with the addition of a long Preface, thus beginning a practice which was to last throughout Shaw's life. Shaw's Prefaces are famous, perhaps even notorious. There have been people who assert that they are better than his plays; but that is nonsense. They do, nevertheless, contain much of his most disturbing and controversial writing, and of his most determined self-justification and self-advertisement. They began by explaining the genesis and expanding the argument of the plays contained in the volume, but tended as Shaw grew older to become more and more discursive, to bang any drum that he wanted, at the moment, banged, and to find ever more instances of the inveterate folly and hopelessness of British institutions.

Many of the instances are the wildest generalizations: for example, in the Preface to *John Bull's Other Island*, one of his most entertaining plays, comparing the English with the Irish, 'It may be,' he wrote, 'that if our (i.e. Ireland's) resources included the armed force and virtually unlimited money which push the political and military figureheads of England through bungled enterprises to a muddled success, and create the illusion of some miraculous and divine innate English quality which enables a general to become a conqueror with abilities that would not suffice to save a cabman from having his licence marked, and a member of parliament to become Prime Minister with the outlook on life of a sporting country solicitor educated by a private governess, I have no doubt we should lapse into gross intellectual sottishness and prefer leaders who encouraged our vulgarities by sharing them, and flattered us by associating them with purchased successes, to our betters.' This is good debating stuff, but hardly shows much sense of history.

Certain playwrights and novelists who in recent years have found the world not to their taste have been nicknamed the Angry Young Men; Shaw, on the contrary, was never quite that, for though he applied the lash indiscriminately to almost everything and everybody in his adopted country, he did so always, until his last years, with a certain gay objectivity and lack of resentment, maintaining at the same time a belief that though Britain and Europe were sunk in a 'gross intellectual sottishness', they were none the less not irretrievably lost, but might one day improve if only they submitted to take the Shavian medicine. Shaw had, that is, positive ideas. The chief of them was that all our troubles, social and personal, are due to stupidity; the common man allows his life to be governed by emotion and prejudice and fails to see things as they are. Now this defect is curable through the lessons of the archangelical schoolmaster, and he begins by giving us hope: there is, he tells us—contrary to the belief of many thinkers today —such a thing as Progress. Man is evolving, and the direction of his evolution is dependent (this is an essential point in Shaw's doctrine) upon his own will. We make ourselves what we wish to be. The giraffe, to repeat the familiar illustration, grew his long neck because he liked the shoots which were high up on the tree. Darwin was wrong; Lamarck and Samuel Butler (the second, after Ibsen, of Shaw's masters) were right. Evolution is not to be explained by natural selection and the survival of the fittest; it is the result of conscious purpose—it is *creative* evolution.

In this Shaw permitted himself a modified optimism; for creative evolution implies that if only men can be brought to see and to desire what is good for them, they will ultimately get it. *How* they will be brought to see and to desire what is good for them will be, we are assured, through an improvement of the intellectual processes. They must stop being silly and confusing fancy with fact, habit with intention, romance with reality. This will take time, as Shaw admitted by writing his Metabiological Pentateuch, *Back to Methuselah*, in which men and women are shown as having willed themselves to prolong their lives to several centuries, in order to acquire more wisdom than can be got in a mere seventy years and to live, all passion spent, in a chilly heaven of pure thought—whatever that may mean. One cannot but wonder what such beings would have left to think about. In point of fact, we have already by improvements in hygiene and nutrition doubled the expectation of life in most European countries during the past hundred years; but it would be rash to say that we have doubled our wisdom.

Another of Shaw's positive ideas was the necessity of political reform. He had a proper and generous horror of the social conditions prevailing at the end of the nineteenth century in England, and well on into the twentieth. How could a society be healthy which tolerated slums and semi-starvation, excessive poverty beside excessive wealth, a labouring class beside a class which lived on unearned money and contributed nothing to the common weal? Most of us can ask such questions with as much urgency as Shaw did; few of us, however, could happily follow him in the actual development of his political ideals. He began, as I have already mentioned, with the Socialism of Sidney Webb and William Morris; then, with a growing passion for regimentation and order, springing from an obstinate refusal to admit the natural diversity of human beings, he turned to Communism. Democratic government in any form he came to hate. He admired Hitler and adulated Stalin. In the Preface to *On the Rocks*, a play written when he was an old man, he wrote that 'extermination must be put on a scientific basis if it is ever to be carried out humanely and apologetically as well as thoroughly.' He had long advocated the extermination of the unfit and of the misfits in an ordered society, as less hypocritical and more effective than punishment or attempted reformation. Once he proposed that every adult man and woman should appear periodically before a tribunal and be ordered to justify his, or her, existence. One trembles to think of whom the tribunal would have consisted and of the standards of judgement they would have adopted. But such things, of course, are mere lunacy; and it is important to realize that there was a good deal of mere lunacy in Shaw, the champion of pure intellect and life-long castigator of muddled thinking. The one virtue of his more appalling absurdities is that they shock us into a clearer perception of the value of their opposites—such things as forgiveness, humility, and the preciousness of the human liberties.

A third positive idea with which Shaw made great play was his substitution of a mysterious entity called the Life Force for the more familiar name of God. He was driven to make the substitution by his refusal to accept a religion which was not intellectually satisfying and intelligible, and by his inability, one supposes, to understand that all creeds are attempts to shadow forth the Inexpressible by such poor symbols as our limited minds are able to hit upon. But symbols would not do for Shaw; he wanted the thing itself, and found it in a vague impersonal Something called the Life Force, which is endlessly seeking its own perfection through the infinite variety of living things, experimenting continually with different forms and throwing on the scrapheap all which prove inadequate to its purpose. Thus one day, if we don't look out, we shall go the way of the dinosaurs and pterodactyls. By far the most entertaining exposition of this idea is in *Man and Superman*, one of the most sparkling and irresistible of all Shaw's plays, both for the sheer fun of it and for the extremely vigorous characterization of Ann Whitefield and of the chauffeur (a newish thing in those days) Enry Straker. The point of the play is to illustrate the working of the Life Force through sexual relationships, and at the same time to explode what Shaw characteristically thought to be the intolerable nonsense of romantic love. Ann knows what she wants: she wants a husband and she wants John Tanner; Tanner knows what he wants —an artist's liberty to 'be himself' and to create. But the Life Force is at work in him as in her; he struggles in vain against what he knows to be his misery yet feels to be his joy. In a rage of defeat he takes Ann in his arms, and Ann, in quiet triumph, submits.

Half-truths can sometimes be more compelling than whole ones, because the dice can be weighted—certainly they are when they are presented with the verve and wit which animate this play, and one cannot admire Shaw the artist too much for the brilliant use he has made of his own emotional weaknesses. It is significant that in most of his plays the women are stronger than the men—and often of the spider kind, eating or preparing to eat their mates. Shaw was in fact afraid of women; for nearly the first thirty years of his life he was too shy to have anything to do with them, and then, suddenly and surprisingly, started vigorous but somewhat anxious flirtations with half a dozen at once. One of them caused him much trouble, even terror, before he could shake her off, and he probably had her in mind when he drew the portrait of the termagant Blanche in *Widowers' Houses* and of the jealous Julia in *The Philanderer*. The sort of love affair which gave him most satisfaction was postal: no-one who had not been told it was true would have believed that half the letters which passed between him and Ellen Terry were written before the two had met. Perhaps the most characteristic of all his preliminary adventures in love was with May Morris, William Morris' daughter, who would have married him had she been asked. Shaw has described the crucial meeting. 'I looked at her,' he wrote, 'rejoicing in the lovely dress and lovely self; and she looked at me very carefully, and quite deliberately made a gesture of assent with her eyes. I was immediately conscious that a Mystic Betrothal was registered in heaven. . . . I did not think it necessary to say anything. It did not occur to me even that fidelity to the Mystic Betrothal need interfere with the ordinary course of my relations with other women. I made no sign at all.' Soon after this incident, apparently to his astonishment, May Morris engaged herself to marry somebody else. When Shaw did finally marry Charlotte Payne-Townshend, it was on the condition, proposed by her, that they should live together as brother and sister. The condition, it seems, was readily accepted, and the two had forty-five years of happy companionship, in mutual trust and deep affection.

All this makes a strange story, which has been told with much understanding and sympathy by St. John Ervine in his admirable biography of Shaw. I have repeated some of the details of it here not from love of literary gossip, but because of the light it throws upon the tone and character of Shaw's work. He was a man with many brilliant gifts; he was the leading entertainer on the London stage—indeed on the world stage—for something like forty years; yet many of us, amused, stimulated, delighted as we are by his work, come back to it nevertheless with a certain uneasiness, a dissatisfaction. In America and Germany as well as in England Shaw has enjoyed an immense popularity; but it is not without significance that in Molière's country his plays have always been received coolly and with a kind of puzzlement. One area of human experience was a closed book to Shaw, and one is constantly aware throughout the long succession of his scintillating comedies of that unread volume. His approach to the problems of life was always the intellectual approach, and led, as it must, to over-simplification of the issues; both of the folly and the grandeur of passion he was unaware, and a little contemptuous. To point this out is not to forget that Shaw was a writer of comedy, or to look for the irrelevant; far from it: the finest comedy, as I have tried elsewhere in this book to indicate, though it may never speak directly of such things, nevertheless springs from a knowledge of them. The fount of Bandusia had gathered its water from the subterranean dark before it bubbled out clear and cool amongst the rocks on Horace's Sabine farm. In a sense, Shaw never really belonged to this world, any more than, as an expatriate Irishman, he belonged to England; his very remoteness from the common run of us all and from the instinctive life which beats in our veins, enabled him to see all the more clearly the quirks of opinion and the obstinate stupidities which confound and mislead us; but at the same time it obscured for him the fact that those obstinate stupidities, those blind starts and ignorant gropings after some will-o'-the-wisp or fantasy of the mind, those dark instinctive movements of the heart towards something we sense but do not understand, are of the very stuff of human character, and indeed of history. In *Caesar and Cleopatra*, one of the finest of Shaw's plays, there is a scene, in the second act, in which the philosopher Theodotus begs Caesar to save the library of Alexandria from the fire which is destroying it. Caesar refuses. 'What is burning there,' cries Theodotus, 'is the memory of mankind.' 'A shameful memory,' Caesar answers; 'let it burn.' 'Will you destroy the past?' 'Ay,' says Caesar, 'and build the future with its ruins.'

Caesar, in this play, is Shaw's picture of the Great Man, as he conceived him, of the man who is the controller of his own destiny and of the world's; yet he makes him incapable of perceiving the obvious fact that without the past the future would be inconceivable and non-existent. To build the future on the ruins of the past is a high-sounding phrase and, in the play, it has its dramatic effect; but it is typical of the half-truths which fell so easily from Shaw's pen. Without the heritage of the past we should be no better than monkeys, with all to do again; the past can never be in ruins, for we carry it with us, and its whole burden of wisdom and folly, glory and shame, in every breath we breathe. There is no *nostrum*, be it Fabian socialism or benevolent dictatorship or conversion to belief in the Life Force and creative evolution, which can give humanity a fresh start; such ideas and others like them, when they are worth anything at all, may be absorbed into, and infinitesimally modify, the vast complex of human experience and endeavour, but the onward movement, if there is one, springs from deeper and more hidden sources.

It is not irrelevant to devote so much attention to Shaw's doctrines and their implications; for though he was a writer of comedy, he was a serious writer and wished to be taken seriously. He was a didactic playwright, and he intended his audiences to laugh themselves into a perception of the truth as he saw it. He was an earnest moral and political reformer, who deliberately adopted the methods of the clown. They are good methods, and to what brilliant use he put them the plays themselves bear witness.

Shaw won no full popular recognition in this country until Granville Barker put on a series of his plays at the Court Theatre from 1904 to 1906. In 1906 Shaw was fifty; he had had a long time to wait for success, but now at last, when it came, it came in a full tide. His plays up to this date included the light-hearted and amusing *You Never Can Tell*—with its hint of the Life Force in the character of poor Valentine the dentist, writhing angry and ecstatic in the toils of his Julia, the almost-impossible twins and the wise old waiter whom every middle-aged character-actor has aspired to play; *Arms and the Man* with its gay satirical comment on the supposed romance and heroism of war; *Candida*, amongst the best of the early plays, and the one which is perhaps least subject to the common critical judgement that Shaw's characters are bundles of characteristics tied together to illustrate a theme rather than living people; *John Bull's Other Island*, with its fresh and penetrating insight into the Irish question; *Major Barbara*, with its skilfully drawn and convincing portrait of the millionaire Andrew Undershaft, its subtly presented discussion of the relationship of means to ends and impressive attack upon poverty as the only vice. Who but

Shaw would have ventured a play for London intellectuals about the Salvation Army and have shown in the course of it real sympathy with the Army's work, in spite of the fact that his own beliefs were diametrically opposed to General Booth's? In addition to these plays there was *Captain Brassbound's Conversion*, *The Devil's Disciple*, and *Man and Superman* of which I have already said something. For sheer quantity alone it was a tremendous output of work, and at the time Shaw was also occupied in the ramifying affairs of the Fabian Society, writing pamphlets and lecturing in its behalf, and—surprisingly—attending with great efficiency to his duties as a vestryman in the Borough of St. Pancras.

All these plays have an extraordinary vitality. I have said enough about Shaw's doctrines to indicate that they had on the whole too little of essential wisdom to count much in the history of thought; but it must never be forgotten that the plays in which he embodied them are, with certain exceptions, masterpieces in their own peculiar kind. It took time for Shaw to 'educate' audiences to appreciate them; but he succeeded, triumphantly. All his plays must be seen to be properly enjoyed; even so acute a critic as Max Beerbohm declared, after reading *Man and Superman*, that it would be intolerable on the stage, and then, having witnessed it, wholeheartedly recanted. This only proves, if proof were needed, that Shaw was a true dramatist, a playwright who instinctively knew his business. His weakest plays are almost always 'good theatre', for he had an incomparable sense of the stage, and knew what would tell. He knew just when and how to shock an audience into attention by a phrase from the streets—'Walk?' says Eliza in *Pygmalion* when asked if she would walk home through the Park, 'not bloody likely!'—and to surprise them into laughter by making his characters utter some sentiment which all of us in ordinary life would have in our minds but few would dare to express. This favourite device of his constantly adds flavour to his dialogue and gives a sense of character sometimes illusory but always effective. Whether his characters are, in the main, bundles of characteristics or not, at least those characteristics are vivid and striking, and his puppets argue themselves into credibility and life—if the phrase may be pardoned—with immense verve and unflagging verbal inventiveness.

By 1914 neither England, in spite of Fabian socialism, nor Europe as a whole had made much progress towards Utopia. Shaw had seen the war coming and had proposed a Four-Power pact, by which any three should combine to crush an aggressor. Like all decent people, Shaw hated war; when it came, it affected him profoundly, and he never again had a prescription to offer for the cure of human ills. His pamphlet *Commonsense about the War*, in which the chief argument was a fierce attack on secret diplomacy and Sir Edward Grey, roused bitter anger, and throughout the war he was looked upon as the enemy and denigrator of everything English. The play, however, which he wrote under the direct stimulus of the war, is amongst his richest and best. This was *Heartbreak House*, a symbolical picture—in the Chekhovian manner, as Shaw described it—of English society brought to the edge of its doom. In the dialogue of this play there is a warmth and earnestness unusual in Shaw: 'Learn your business as an Englishman,' says Captain Shotover, the eccentric prophet. 'And what,' asks the bewildered Hector, 'may my business as an Englishman be, pray?' 'Navigation,' answers Shotover. 'Learn it and live; or leave it and be damned.' *Heartbreak House* was published in 1919 with a comminatory preface which added nothing to its effect. It was not acted in London until 1921, when it failed, though in the previous year it had been well received in New York.

Shaw's first major work after the war was *Back to Methuselah*, of which I have already said something. Implicit in it, as in most of Shaw's work, is the notion of creative evolution, which he first developed so amusingly and persuasively in *Man and Superman*—and the cognate idea of the battle of the sexes between Man the Artist and Woman the Mother. Shaw thought *Back to Methuselah* his best play, but few have agreed with him. It takes five days to perform. Most people, I fancy, would give the first place amongst Shaw's plays to *Saint Joan*, which he wrote at the suggestion of his wife, when he was seventy. It was probably his most successful play from its first performance, with Sybil Thorndike as the Maid, onward, and it has since been revived more often than any other. It has all Shaw's techincal mastery and brilliance, and there are passages in it—a rare thing in Shaw's work—which are deeply moving. 'Old Shaw,' I remember a friend of mine saying to me, 'has at last fallen in love.' The Maid herself is a credible and beautiful character, and few who have seen, or even only read, the play will forget the astonishing *tour de force* of the Inquisitor's speech on heresy (no playwright but Shaw could have held an audience's attention through a closely reasoned speech of such length), or Joan's passionate outburst when she learns that her judges will spare her the stake only to imprison her for life:

> You promised me life, but you lied. You think that life is nothing but not being stone dead. It is not the bread and water I fear.... Bread has no sorrow for me and water no affliction. But to shut me out from the light of the sky and the sight of the fields and flowers; to chain my feet so that I can never again ride with the soldiers nor climb the hills; to make me breathe foul damp darkness and keep from me everything that brings me back to the love of God when your wickedness and foolishness tempt me to hate Him: all this is worse than the furnace in the Bible that was heated seven times.
>
> I could do without my warhorse; I could drag about in a skirt... if only I could still hear the wind in the trees, the larks in the sunshine, the young lambs crying through the healthy frost, and the blessed, blessed, church bells that send my angel voices floating to me on the wind. But without these things I cannot live; and by your wanting to take them away from me, or from any human creature, I know that your counsel is of the devil, and that mine is of God.

Shaw's exclusively intellectual activities quickly overlaid his feeling for nature: he cared little where he lived; he disliked his home at Ayot St. Lawrence but never bothered to move elsewhere, and foreign travel bored him; but in these words which he put into Joan's mouth he seems, to me at any rate, to have returned for a moment in memory to his childhood days when he went for the first time to live in Torca Cottage in Dalkey on Killiney Bay, and delighted in his freedom from the Dublin streets. The words humanize Shaw for me; yet my friend exaggerated when he said that Shaw had at last fallen in love. He never quite did that. *Saint Joan*, like all the plays, was published with a Preface: it is a fine play, but I am told that the experts in theology and medievalism consider the preface to be childish.

Shaw wrote many more plays which I have not space to mention, though I should have liked to say something about the charming *Androcles and the Lion*, and the effective anti-democratic political piece *The Apple Cart*, into which (to venture a small scrap of literary gossip) he introduced a ludicrous incident from his own experience. Shaw was always punctilious about keeping even the slightest promise he had made to his wife, and one evening when he had been visiting Mrs. Patrick Campbell he duly rose from his seat as the clock struck six, that being the hour at which he had told Mrs. Shaw he would return. Mrs. Campbell demurred, but Shaw insisted; she urged him to remain, but Shaw shook his head. Finally she seized him by the lapel of his coat, and in the ensuing struggle they both fell to the floor—just at the moment when a servant opened the door and looked in. A similar scene takes place in *The Apple Cart* between King Magnus and Orinthia. It is hard, too, not to mention *Fanny's First Play*, and that wholly delightful piece of nonsense, the curtain-raiser *How he Lied to her Husband*.

Of Shaw's last plays I am glad not to have room to speak. His disillusionment about society had begun with the First World War; it grew and deepened, until in his old age it had become something like despair. That is the fate of all reformers who believe that *notions* will change the world. *On the Rocks* is a barren and querulous piece, and there were plays—like *Geneva*—in which Shaw's adulation of such men as Mussolini becomes intolerable. Yet Shaw was a great writer; for sheer quantity his work is almost without parallel except amongst the second-rate. Apart from over fifty plays and his immense and varied political activities, he found time to write a critical study of Ibsen, another of Wagner, and two very long political treatises, the better known of which is *The Intelligent Woman's Guide to Socialism and Capitalism.* He continued to work almost to the day of his death.

In 1937 he fell ill with pernicious anaemia, but recovered. Six years later his wife died, and her death left him desolate. He had outlived nearly all his friends—Archer, Chesterton, Webb being the dearest of them. He was still writing—the book was *Everybody's Political What's What.* He had little left to live for; for he had loved his friends, and he had loved his wife. But his unquenchable vitality carried him on a little longer. He who had been the clever young man, regarded with unwilling admiration and some mistrust, the middle-aged castigator of English institutions who had made himself well hated in the first war, now at last, and to his amused surprise, found himself the object of universal affection and respect. He had already received the Nobel Prize for literature—and had refused the Order of Merit. In 1949 he published *Sixteen Self Sketches,* only a few of which had been previously written; some of the Sketches are a little shrill in self-defence, but one would never guess, if one did not know, that they were the work of so old a man. The following year he tripped while he was pruning fruit trees in his garden at Ayot, and broke a leg. He died on November 2nd at the age of ninety-four.

A book of this kind, if it is to be of any interest, cannot be impersonal. I have tried in the course of it to suggest certain principles which I think should be borne in mind when we try to determine what qualities distinguish great drama from good drama—not to mention the second-rate. I have made it clear, I suppose, that I do not love Shaw as I love certain of the other playwrights whose work I have described; but what I deprecate, others may admire. Shaw was an incomparable entertainer and showman, and the fact that he made the stage, in America and Europe as well as in our own country, once again a vehicle of serious, even though erroneous, philosophical ideas, was a service to the drama which should never be forgotten.

Suggestions for further reading

SHAKESPEARE

Sir Edmund Chambers: *William Shakespeare.*
J. W. MacKail: *The Approach to Shakespeare.*
John Masefield: *William Shakespeare.*
Sir A. Quiller-Couch: *Shakespeare's Workmanship.*
Logan Pearsall Smith: *On Reading Shakespeare.*
F. E. Halliday: *Shakespeare and His Critics.*

SOPHOCLES

Special studies assume more knowledge than is possessed by beginners. For future reading I would recommend general studies of Greek life and thought: e.g. H. D. F. Kitto: *The Greeks*; also his *Greek Dramatists*; Haigh's *Attic Theatre* contains a mass of useful information. The translation by E. F. Watling of the seven plays in the Penguin Classics is valuable.

MOLIÈRE

Martin Turnell: *The Classical Moment.*
D. B. Wyndham Lewis: *Molière: The Comic Mask.*

Not much has been written in English about Molière. I would recommend to venturesome readers Meredith's essay, *The Comic Spirit*, which, for all its mannerisms, is a fine piece of work. The classic French assessment of Molière is Sainte-Beuve's essay in *Portraits Littéraires.*

SHERIDAN

Walter Sichel: *Life of Sheridan.*

Charles Lamb: *On the Artificial Comedy of the Last Century* (Essays of Elia).

IBSEN

Professor Koht: *Life of Ibsen.*

G. B. Shaw: *The Quintessence of Ibsenism.*

Janko Lavrin: *Ibsen: an Approach.*

M. C. Bradbrook: *Ibsen the Norwegian.*

SHAW

St. John Ervine: *Bernard Shaw.*

Hesketh Pearson: *G. B. S. A Postscript.*